D1014611

AN ILLUSTRATED GUIDE TO THE

MODERN SOVIET NAVY

Published by Arco Publishing, Inc.
NEW YORK

AN ILLUSTRATED GUIDE TO THE MODERN SOVIET NAVY

John Jordan

A Salamander Book

Published by
Arco Publishing, Inc.,
219 Park Avenue South,
New York,
N.Y. 10003,
United States of America.

Library of Congress catalog card number 81-71939

ISBN 0-668-05504-9

All correspondence concerning the content of this volume should be addressed to Salamander Books Ltd.

Credits

Author: John Jordan is a contributor to many important defense journals, a consultant to the Soviet section of 1980-81 "Jane's Fighting Ships", and co-author of Salamander's "Balance of Military Power".

Photographs supplied by Captain J.E. Moore, RN, US Navy, British MoD, Ambrose Greenway and Reportagebild.
Project manager: Ray Bonds.
Editors: Richard O'Neill; Philip de Ste. Croix.
Designer: Philip Gorton.
Line drawings: © Siegfried Breyer and © John Jordan.
Diagrams: **TIGA** © Salamander Books Ltd.
Filmset: Modern Text Typesetting Ltd.
Printed in Belgium by Henri Proost et Cie.

Contents

Organisation of the Soviet Surface Navy

The development of the Soviet Navy has been dominated by two factors. The first is the lack of any historical naval tradition outside the Baltic and the Black Sea. The second, intimately linked with the first, is the adverse maritime geography of the USSR, a large continental land-mass with limited access to the open oceans. Both the history and the geography of the Soviet Union have dictated that the major fighting force should be the Army, latterly backed up by a large land-based Air Force.

Until the early 1960s the entire *raison d'être* of the Navy was to protect those fringes of the Soviet land-mass that were vulnerable to assault from the sea. The Navy's tasks were, therefore: territorial defence against bombardment and amphibious assault; area defence against incursions into Soviet sea-space by enemy surface units and submarines; and reinforcement and support of the Army. These missions motivated the massive construction programme based on cruisers, destroyers and medium-range submarines on which the Soviet Navy embarked in the immediate postwar period.

Khrushchev's accession to full power in 1955 prompted a fundamental reappraisal of the kind of forces needed to carry out Soviet naval missions, but the missions themselves remained the same. Thus, although the programme of conventional cruisers and destroyers was dramatically curtailed, it was because their mission of area defence against Western amphibious forces and carrier task forces was now to be performed by

Above: Admiral Gorshkov, the father of the modern Soviet Navy.

ships armed with cruise missiles. Similar developments curtailed the submarine programme: Whiskey class boats were fitted with long-range SS-N-3 missiles as an interim measure while Soviet designers hastily prepared plans for purpose-built missile submarines. (Soviet submarines receive full coverage in a companion volume: *An Illustrated Guide to Modern Submarines,* Salamander Books, 1982).

A large force of land-based bombers, also armed with long-range anti-ship missiles, was built up. This was to combine with the new missile-armed surface ships and submarines to defend Soviet seaspace against incursions by NATO carrier task forces, which now possessed a nuclear strike capability. The revolution in naval construction instituted under Krushchev was, however, a revolution in technology, not in basic strategy.

The ASW Programme

The factor which changed everything was the development of the Polaris missile-armed submarine, which first entered service with the US Navy in 1960-61. By the mid-1960s the US had a massive SSBN programme in full swing: 13 Polaris boats were completed in 1964 alone. The threat to Soviet territory shifted from the (NATO) carriers to submarines operating outside Soviet sea-space. The 1,500nm (2,775 km) radius of the early A-1 and A-2 missiles, together with the acquisition by the US Navy of basing rights in Rota, Spain, and Holy Loch, Scotland, suggested launch points in the Norwegian Sea, the northern reaches of the North Sea, and the Eastern Mediterranean—all areas outside the traditional sphere of Soviet naval operations.

The Soviet Navy responded by instituting a massive programme of antisubmarine construction and by commencing regular deployments to the threat areas. Cruisers which were to have carried anti-ship missiles were ▶

Soviet Construction Programmes

Surface Ships	*Submarines*
Post-War Programme (1946-1958)	
14 Sverdlov *(KR)*	32 Zulu *(PLD)*
64 Skory *(EM)*	200 Whiskey *(PL)*
27 Kotlin *(EM)*	
Anti-Carrier Programme (1956-1965)	
4 Kildin *(RK)**	7 Zulu V *(PLRB)*
8 Krupny *(RK)**	11 Whiskey T.C./Long Bin *(PLRK)*
4 Kynda *(RKR)*	29 Golf *(PLRB)*
4 Kresta I *(RKR)*	9 Hotel *(PLARB)*
20 Kashin *(BPK)*	16 Juliett *(PLRK)*
	34 Echo I/II *(PLARK)*
	60 Foxtrot *(PLD)*
	14 November *(PLA)*
**denotes conversion*	20 Romeo *(PL)*
ASW Programme (1962-1978)	
2 Moskva *(PKR)*	34 Yankee *(PLARB)*
2 (+2) Kiev *(PKR)*	33 Delta *(PLARB)*
10 Kresta II *(BPK)*	16 Charlie *(PLARK)*
7 Kara *(BPK)*	28 Victor *(PLA)*
29 Krivak I/II *(BPK)*	15 Tango *(PLD)*
	4 Alfa *(PLA)*
Balanced Fleet Programme (1975 onwards)	
1 (+1) Kirov *(RKR)*	1 (+?) Typhoon *(PLARB)*
1 (+3) BlackCom 1 *(RKR?)*	1 (+?) Oscar *(PLARK)*
1 (+3) Sovremenny *(BRK)*	
1 (+3) Udaloy *(BPK)*	

Note: equivalent Western designations for submarines;

PLRB—SBB: PLRK—SSG: PL/PLD—SS: PLARB—SSBN: PLARK—SSGN: PLA—SSN.

(For an explanation of Soviet surface ship classification, see Introductions to sub-sections of book).

▶ redesigned with antisubmarine weapons; destroyers originally built as Rocket Ships were rebuilt as Large Antisubmarine Ships; and a specialist ASW helicopter was developed for operation from larger vessels, including two new helicopter carriers.

There were major changes in the relative status of the four Soviet fleets. The Baltic Fleet, traditionally the most important, retained its accustomed role as a coastal defence force. The Northern Fleet, based in the hostile, ice-bound Arctic, received most of the new ocean-going ASW units and nearly all of the latest nuclear-powered submarines, because of its relatively unrestricted access to the open oceans. The Black Sea Fleet would have gone into a decline similar to that of the Baltic Fleet had it not been the obvious candidate to provide the growing squadron of major vessels in the Mediterranean, which now usually included one of the helicopter carriers. Significantly, the Pacific Fleet, one of the major beneficiaries of the construction programme of the 1950s, was now starved of modern ocean-going vessels.

In totally altering the balance of Soviet naval missions, two major technical difficulties had to be faced. The first was the primitive nature of Soviet ASW technology, which had received a very low priority in the postwar period. (In contrast, the West, faced by a large Soviet submarine construction programme, had made enormous strides in underwater detection). The second was the problem of effective defence against attack from the air while operating outside Soviet sea-space.

During the 1950s the Soviet Navy had chosen not to develop aircraft carriers, partly because of the massive expenditure involved in building up a seaborne air capability from scratch and the effect such an undertaking would have on the programmes of the Soviet Air Force, but also because Soviet naval missions did not at that time require them.

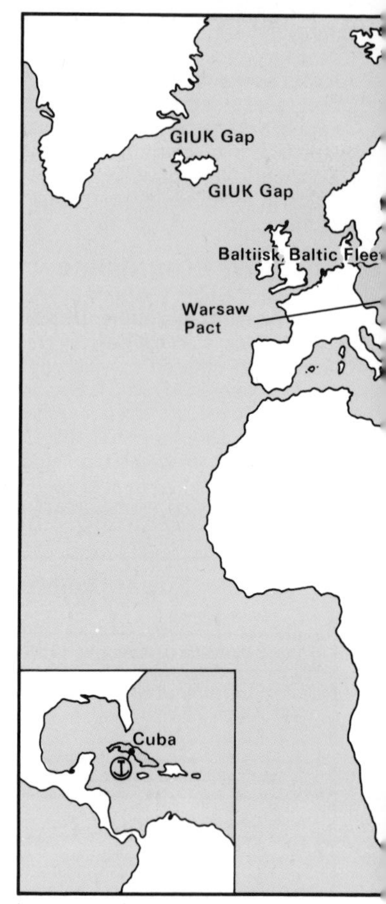

It was envisaged that the great land-mass of the Soviet Union would be a single giant aircraft carrier, with mobility assured by the rapid transfer of air squadrons around an extensive network of air bases on its borders. Surface forces and submarines defending Soviet sea-space would thus have a protective land-based air umbrella and would attack their opponents in conjunction with land-based bombers armed, like the naval units, with anti-ship missiles.

To resolve the ASW problem, the Soviet Navy embarked on a programme of massive investment in sonar technology. Soviet sonars of the 1950s had been high-frequency (ie, short-range) "searchlight" types, scarcely more advanced than those employed by the US Navy and Royal

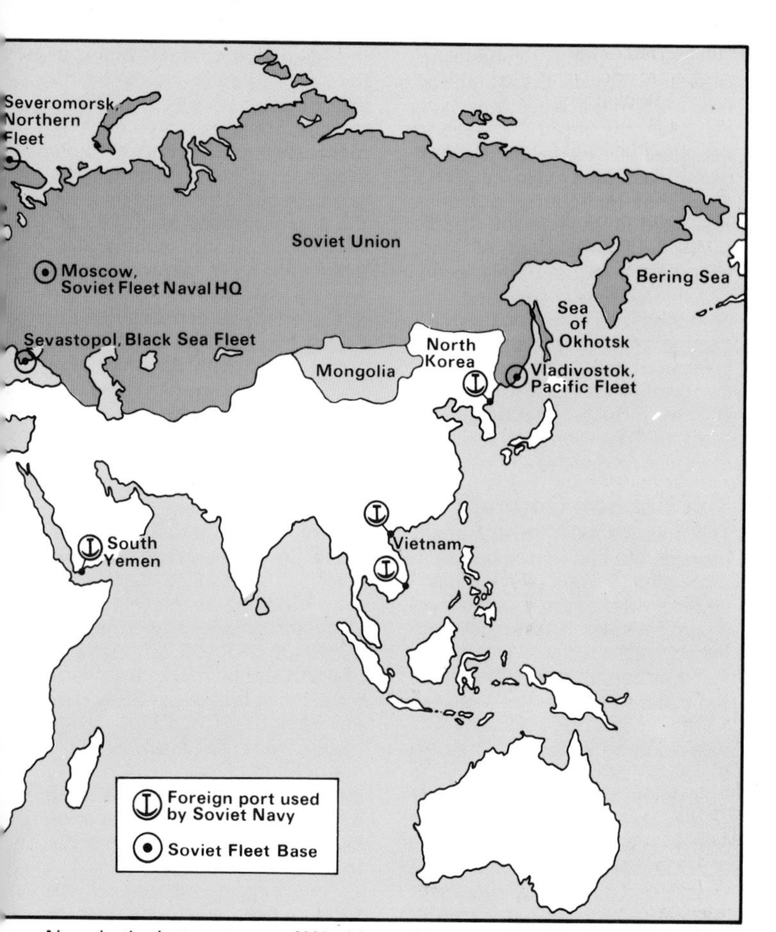

Above: Soviet naval activity now extends worldwide. This map shows fleet bases.

Navy in the latter stages of World War II. But by the time the helicopter cruiser *Moskva* was completed in 1967-68 the Soviets had produced a low-frequency panoramic sonar of adequate power and range for use in conjunction with antisubmarine missiles. The development of sonars of all types and sizes, including medium and low-frequency bow-mounted models, independent variable depth sonars and dipping sonars to be used on helicopters and small craft, proceeded at a dramatic rate. (Data processing, however, continues to lag behind Western capabilities).

The problem of air defence without carriers was more difficult to resolve. Although the limitations inherent in a "land-based" maritime strategy were now apparent, the Soviet Chiefs of Staff were as yet unwilling to concede that sea-based air was essential to open-ocean operations. The solutions adopted were, therefore, an extension of previous policy. All Soviet ocean-going units would henceforth be liberally equipped with defensive AAW systems: area defence surface-to-air missiles; close-in anti-missile systems such as the 30mm gatling; and an extensive range of powerful ECM jammers.

The "offensive" mission—performed for the West by the carrier attack squadrons—would be assumed by a new class of submarine (Charlie), armed with short-range "pop-up" missiles. ▶

▶Unlike previous submarine-launched missiles, these could be fired when the boat was submerged, enabling the Charlie to get close to its target without being detected. No external source of mid-course guidance was needed, making the Charlie relatively independent of land-based air. It required only reconnaissance data regarding the composition and location of enemy task groups; this, it was envisaged, would be provided by the Tupolev Tu-20 (NATO: "Bear D") long-range recce-bomber, specially equipped with a variety of detection devices.

The Bastion Concept

The massive ASW re-equipment programme had hardly begun to take effect when Soviet naval strategy had to be modified yet again to meet further developments.

It was becoming apparent that the attempt to counter Western SSBNs with open-ocean ASW was doomed to failure. The new Soviet ships met with conspicuous lack of success in their efforts to detect submarines on patrol—and the advent of the 2,500nm (4,625 km) Polaris A-3 missile and its MIRVed successor Poseidon increased the area of potential SSBN operations out of all proportion to the increase in missile range.

The other factor was the breakthrough made by the West in underwater surveillance. The development of SOSUS, an extensive network of hydrophones on the sea-bed at strategic points in the North Atlantic and the northern Pacific, enabled NATO to monitor Soviet submarine movements through the choke-points they had to cross to reach the open oceans. This made possible the establishment of ASW barriers, comprising submarines, dedicated ASW surface groups and LRMP aircraft. Since the entire offensive capability of the Soviet Navy in the open-ocean areas rested with its long-range nuclear submarine fleet, this was a very serious development: not only the SSNs and SSGNs, but also the SSBNs, including the latest Yankee class boats, would have to cross these barriers in order to carry out their missions.

The Soviet Navy reacted in two ways. Later Yankee class hulls were modified as the Delta class to accommodate a new ballistic missile, the SS-N-8, with a range of 4,200nm (7,770 km)—nearly three times that of the SS-N-6 on the Yankees. The Deltas, completed from 1973 onward, did not need to cross Western ASW barriers: the range of the SS-N-8 is such that its carrier submarine barely has to put to sea in order to fire it!

The primary mission of the surface fleet would henceforth be the support of Soviet submarine operations. Delta SSBNs would be grouped in holding areas, or "bastions", in the Barents Sea and the Sea of Okhotsk, guarded by Soviet ASW forces against incursions by NATO attack submarines.

The "offensive" aspect involved Soviet surface forces operating in conjunction with submarines and the new long-range Tupolev Tu-26 "Backfire" bombers to break up the NATO ASW barrier in the Greenland—Iceland—UK (GIUK) Gap, thus facilitating the safe transit of Soviet attack and cruise-missile submarines. This resulted in new emphasis on anti-ship capabilities, such as the 24 long-range SS-N-12 missiles carried by the new ASW cruisers of the Kiev class and the subsequent construction of the Kirov class "battle-cruisers" as the focal point of Surface Action Groups (SAGs). Tactical considerations dictated that in the North Atlantic area the Soviet Navy must be able effectively to contest the entire Norwegian Sea area, as far west as Iceland. Western task forces were to be overwhelmed by saturation missile attacks launched from above and below the surface.

To coordinate the three elements of the anti-carrier "trad", an extensive network of Bear B recce-bombers and satellites would monitor the movements of hostile naval forces in a system

Left: The SS-N-8 missile of this Delta II-class SSBN can reach the major cities of the United States from sea areas close to Soviet bases.

Above: Air-capable ships such as *Kiev* have added a new dimension to Soviet naval operations. A Yak-36 Forger is visible on the flight deck.

known to the West as the Soviet Ocean Surveillance System (SOSS).

The resultant command structure had two features which appealed to Soviet political and military doctrine: it was emphatically centralized and it was land-based. The naval units involved in an operation would be instructed where to go and when to fire, and would be given only as much of the overall tactical picture as was necessary for the performance of their individual missions. (Few Soviet ships are fitted with the large, expensive tactical data systems of their NATO counterparts). To Western thinking such a system has two major weaknesses: it stifles the initiative of individual commanders and it makes vulnerable the lines of communication.

New Developments

There is every indication that the West is currently witnessing yet another fundamental shift in Soviet naval strategy. It is reported that materials are being assembled for the construction of a 60,000-ton, nuclear-powered aircraft carrier. Experimental test-▶

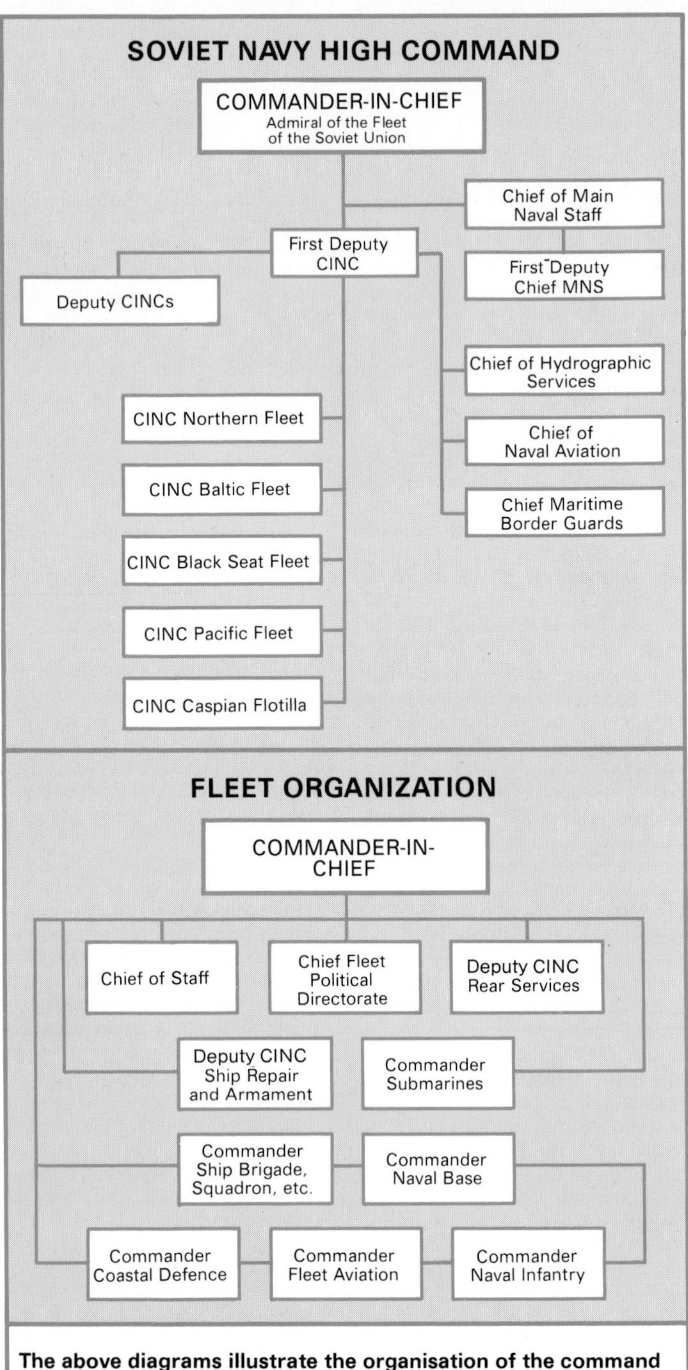

The above diagrams illustrate the organisation of the command structure of the Soviet Navy. For nearly 25 years Admiral Sergei Gorshkov has held the highest office in the Soviet Navy: that of Commander-in-Chief.

▶ ing of steam catapults has taken place, and navalised versions of the MiG-23/27 "Flogger" have been suggested as possible candidates for the new carrier's air group. The timing of the decision to build this vessel has been placed around 1974; it apparently followed fierce debates within the higher echelons of the Soviet Armed Forces.

If the report proves true, the Soviet Navy will, for the first time, have a capability for truly independent operations (ie, without the support of land-based air). It will also, ironically, be an admission that previous attempts to "by-pass" the aircraft carrier by concentrating development on missile and satellite technology have not been satisfactory, and that the Soviets regard the fleet which they built up during the 1960s and 1970s to be limited in its operational capabilities by the absence of integral air support.

The problems that the Soviets will encounter in developing a true aircraft carrier will be their total lack of experience of conventional fixed-wing operations (all of *Kiev's* aircraft take off and land vertically), and the provision of suitable aircraft. The only types mentioned so far are land-based fighter-bombers—and the West's adaptation of land-based types for carrier use has not been very successful.

There are further signs of a shift in Soviet naval strategy. Whereas major Soviet ship-types of the 1960-80 period were essentially self-sufficient—ie, they were designed for single-ship operations and were expected to deal with both surface and sub-surface threats without the assistance of other units—two new classes which emerged in the early 1980s displayed many of the "specialist" features of Western warship construction. *Sovremenny,* lead ship of the first of these classes, is designed primarily for surface action and is equipped with long-range anti-ship missiles and large-calibre guns. *Udaloy,* on the other hand, is a dedicated ASW destroyer remarkably similar in size and capabilities to the US Navy's Spruance class. Both the new Soviet classes are to be armed with medium-range surface-to-air missiles, but *Udaloy* has no anti-ship weapons and the antisubmarine capability of *Sovremenny* is minimal.

To a certain extent, these two types merely consolidate the experiences of the Soviet Navy over the past two decades, confirming the division in concept and mission between the ASW Ship and the Rocket Ship; but it is important to note that their construction raises the possibility of balanced task forces: surface action groups (SAGs) protected against submarines by specialist ASW ships; sub-hunting groups protected against enemy surface units by specialist Rocket Ships; and carrier battle groups which will include both types.

Current Capabilities and Limitations

The development of the world's second most powerful fleet has not changed the fundamental geographical disadvantages under which that fleet has to operate. Not only are Soviet ports in all fleet areas except the Black Sea subject to severe icing for several months in the year; but also the four Soviet fleets can easily be isolated from one another and, in the event of hostilities, they would almost certainly have to operate as independent units.

All major surface warships in the Northern Fleet were built in shipyards in the Baltic or the Black Sea and return to those yards even for routine refitting. It would, however, be an easy matter for NATO to close the straits which separate Denmark from Norway. The surface ships of the Soviet Mediterranean Squadron are generally provided by the Black Sea Fleet—and the closure of the Bosphorus would effectively bottle up the Black Sea Fleet and prevent the ships serving in the Mediterranean from returning to their home ▶

Above: The Soviet Navy relies heavily on conscription in order to man its ships.

▶ bases. The operational area of the Pacific Fleet, with the exception of the ice-bound and isolated submarine base at Petropavlovsk, is totally enclosed by the Japanese islands.

The Soviet Navy has traditionally been strong in coastal operations; in particular, in the use of mining to protect its own harbours, in guarding the flanks of the Army against amphibious assault, and in generally restricting the movement of enemy surface traffic. Most small Soviet ships, including minesweepers, are equipped for minelaying, and even large modern units such as the Krivaks are fitted with mine rails.

Open-ocean capabilities are, however, still limited by the lack of seaborne air. Failure to develop aircraft carriers means that surface units operating out of area are vulnerable to attack from NATO carrier battle groups; even those units equipped with long-range cruise missiles are outranged by carrier strike aircraft such as the A-6 Intruder and A-7 Corsair. The land-based reconnaissance and missile relay aircraft on which Soviet surface units depend could not hope to operate unscathed in close proximity to the NATO carrier battle groups. Therefore, the ability of Soviet ships to perform their missions depends on taking out the US Navy's carriers in the early stages of a conflict. The chances of achieving this in the all-important North Atlantic area diminish with distance (ie, Soviet anti-carrier capabilities are greatest in the northern reaches of the Norwegian Sea and decline significantly the farther south and west the carriers operate).

Another result of Soviet failure to develop the aircraft carrier is the lack of a power-projection capability. The VTOL aircraft of the Kievs can be used to support ground troops and amphibious landings, but the Soviet Navy will not be able to conduct sustained ship-to-shore air strikes until the advent, if such is planned, of the new carrier.

Similarly, there has been no attempt to build up an ocean-going amphibious fleet. Soviet landing ships have an average displacement of 1,000 to 4,000 tons, compared with 8,000 to 11,000 tons for their US Navy counterparts. Only the new *Ivan Rogov* can operate helicopters and landing-craft and the Soviet Naval Infantry has no integral air support comparable to that of the US Marines. Soviet amphibious missions must be seen in the context of support of the Army; landings over relatively short distances are envisaged, with a seaborne assault on the flanks of the enemy complemented by paratroop landings. The major Soviet amphibious forces are based in the Baltic and the Black Sea, where their probable mission would be the seizure of the respective straits.

Open-ocean capabilities are also inhibited by a totally inadequate force of underway replenishment ships. Some effort has been made over the past decade to provide modern vessels able to transfer large quantities of oil and other liquid stores, but dry-store transfer capacity is much inferior to that of the Royal Navy, which has only a fraction of the number of ocean-going surface units. Soviet warships on deployment must rely heavily on replenishment at anchorages which would surely be denied them in the event of hostilities.

The Soviet Navy's heavy dependence on conscription, and the consequent effect on ship- and weapon-philosophy, must be seen as a major weakness. Technical training is sketchy and retention rates are poor, resulting in a chronic shortage of well-qualified personnel. Soviet ships spend little time at sea compared with their Western counterparts; even those on deployment spend most of the time at anchor. Frequent breakdowns — some serious — in equipment occur, and most maintenance work appears to be performed by workmen operating at shore bases.

Soviet ship-philosophy envisages reliance on numbers rather than technical sophistication—another consequence of conscript manning. On corvettes and coastal vessels, massed ASW mortars compensate for the absence of precision-guided weapons. Major warships undergo no mid-life modernization and become obsolete quicker than their Western counterparts. Nevertheless, many are retained when they would long have been discarded by Western navies, in order to provide sea training for conscripts and as a substantial "reserve" force to back up first-line units.

There is evidence of considerable change; indications that the Soviet Navy has learned much from its experience of open-ocean operations over the past fifteen years. The Soviet postwar surface fleet has been beset by constant changes of direction. Its construction and development programmes have often been devised too hastily, in response to Western developments. There are, however, signs that with the new ship classes now entering service the Soviet Navy is finally reaching its maturity.

Below: The Soviet Naval Infantry serves as an advance force for the Soviet Army. Naval air support is limited.

Ocean-Going Ships

Soviet fleet units in the immediate postwar period continued to employ traditional classifications. The Soviet term for cruiser was *Kreyser* (abbreviated to KR); and for destroyer, *Eskadrenny Minonosets* (EM).

With the advent of missile armament, however, the Soviet Navy wisely abandoned the old classifications and introduced a new system more responsive to the fundamental changes in conception and mission of their new warships. (In the West the old system of classification was retained; the result has been considerable confusion, especially in the destroyer and frigate categories.)

The first Soviet fleet missile units were divided into Rocket Ships (Kildin and Krupny) classes) and Rocket Cruisers (Kynda class), all with a primary

Below: An overhead of *Minsk,* the second of the Kiev-class Antisubmarine Cruisers. The unusual configuration shows the extent to which the Soviet Navy is prepared to innovate.

anti-surface mission. In 1963-64, however, the dramatic re-orientation of Soviet naval missions towards ASW operations brought with it two important new categories: the Large Antisubmarine Ship (Kashin, Kanin and Kresta classes) and the Antisubmarine Cruiser (Moskva class).

The resultant system of classification, which has been developed and refined and now embraces coastal vessels as well as the larger fleet units, has proved both logical and flexible. Ships are classified according to mission—Rocket (= anti-surface)/Antisubmarine—and according to size—Cruiser/Large Ship/ Small Ship.

It is important to note that the Soviet Navy does not have an anti-air warfare (AAW) mission, for neither Carrier Battle Group defence nor the protection of large mercantile convoys enter into current Soviet operational concepts. It is for this reason that I have deliberately chosen to use the word "Rocket" in preference to "Missile" as a translation of the Russian word *Raketny,* in order to avoid confusion with the Western terms "Guided-Missile Cruiser" (CG) and "Guided-Missile Destroyer" (DDG), which are used to denote ships whose primary mission is anti-air, not anti-surface, warfare.

The basic system of classification applied to Soviet ocean-going vessels is as follows:

ASW Ships

Protivolodochny Kreyser (ASW Cruiser/PKR), equipped with antisubmarine helicopter squadrons; *Bol'shoy Protivolodochny Korabl'* (Large ASW Ship/BPK), armed with antisubmarine missiles and/or mortars and/or helicopter.

Rocket Ships

Raketny Kreyser (Rocket Cruiser/ RKR), armed with long-range anti-ship missiles;
Bol'shoy Raketny Korabl' (Large Rocket Ship/BRK), armed with medium/horizon-range anti-ship missiles.

Two classes included in this section do not fit exactly into either the new or the old system of classification.

The first is the Krivak, which started life as a BPK but in 1977-78 was reclassified as a Patrol Ship (SKR), traditionally a designation only applied to coastal and area defence vessels (see Introduction, pages 76-77.). The Krivak class is included here because it is essentially an ocean-going vessel; the change in classification simply reflects the extension of the Soviet area defence concept to include ocean areas.

The second is the Sverdlov-Mod. class, which after conversion received the designation *Korabl' Upravleniye* (Command Ship/KRU).

Top right: The Antisubmarine Cruiser *Moskva.*

Right: The conventional cruiser *Aleksandr Suvorov.*

Below: Two BPKs of the Kashin class in the Mediterranean.

857

AIRCRAFT-CARRYING CRUISER/TAKR

Kiev

Completed: 1975 onward, Nikolayev South.
Names: *Kiev, Minsk, Novorossisk* (+ 1 building).
Displacement: 36,000t standard; 42,000t full load.
Dimensions: 899 oa x 157 x 33ft (274 x 48 x 10m).
Propulsion: 4-shaft geared steam turbines; 180,000shp = 32kt.
Armament: *Aircraft:* 12 Yak-36 Forger VTOL; 18-21 Hormone A and B helicopters.
ASW: twin SUW-N-1 launcher (20 ? missiles);
two RBU 6000 mortars;
ten 21in (533mm) TT (2x5).
AAW: two twin SA-N-3 launchers (72 missiles);
two twin SA-N-4 launchers (36 missiles); four 76mm (2x2);
eight 30mm gatlings.
SSM: Eight SS-N-12 launchers (24 missiles).
Sensors: *Surveillance:* Top Sail, Top Steer.
Precision Approach: Top Knot.
Fire Control: two Head Lights, two Pop Group, two Owl Screech, four Bass Tilt.
Sonars: LF bow sonar, VDS.

The Kiev class aircraft-carrying cruisers are currently the largest Soviet ships in service. Although they were developed from the Moskva class, a more conventional flight deck arrangement was adopted to enable the ship to operate fixed-wing VTOL aircraft as well as helicopter squadrons. The forward part, however, remains that of a cruiser, giving *Kiev* and her sisters a unique carrier/cruiser configuration, without parallel in the West.

The primary mission of the Kiev class is ASW, and for this they carry an outfit of weapon systems almost identical to that of the Moskva class: 15-18 Hormone A helicopters; an SUW-N-1 launcher forward for FRAS-1 missiles; ▶

Below: Profile and plan views of the Kiev class. Note the carrier/cruiser configuration with the cruiser weapons shared between the forecastle and the island structure.

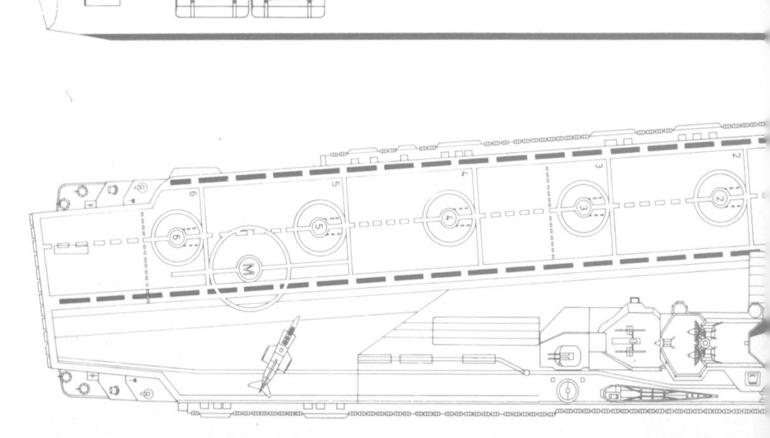

Above: This bow shot of *Kiev* shows clearly the large battery of antiship missiles on the forecastle. The hybrid carrier/cruiser configuration is also evident.

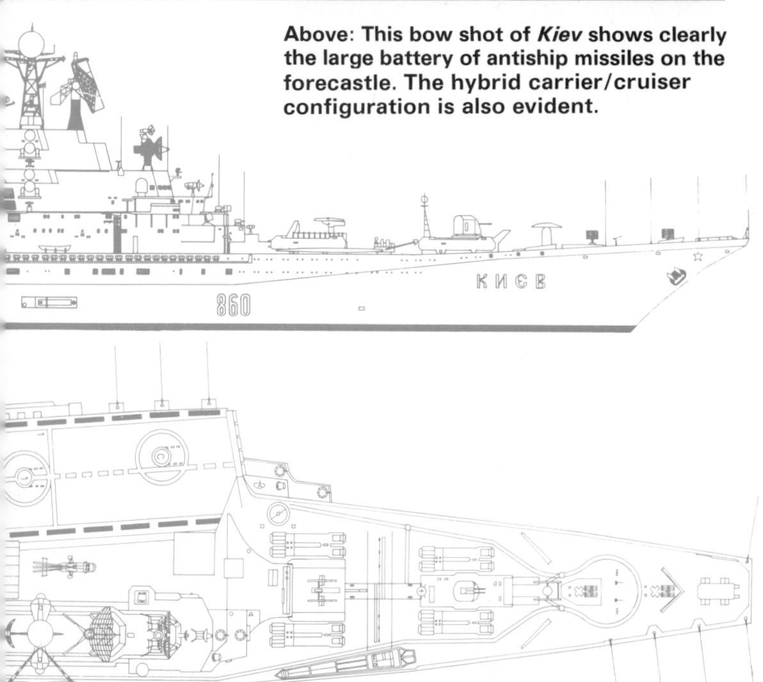

▶ and the customary complement of mortars and torpedo tubes. Target data are provided by a large low-frequency bow sonar and a variable depth sonar.

The principal AAW system, the SA-N-3, is also that of *Moskva,* although the layout of *Kiev's* launchers--one is located at the after end of the island superstructure, thereby covering the after arcs--is clearly more satisfactory. The missile itself may be an improved model with increased range, and it is thought that magazine capacity may have also been increased. The other major AAW weapons are disposed in similar fashion: a twin 76mm mounting on the forecastle with a second on the after end of the superstructure; an SA-N-4 "bin" on the port side of the forecastle with a second on the starboard side of the island. Finally, there are groups of two gatlings, together with a Bass Tilt director, in all four "quadrants" of the ship; the forward groups are mounted on a sponson to port and at the forward end of the superstructure respectively.

In terms of ASW and AAW weapon systems, *Kiev* can therefore be said to correspond to the Kara-class BPK in the same way that *Moskva* corresponds to the Kresta II. The considerable increase in size and capability as compared to *Moskva* is accounted for by two major new elements: long-range SSMs and VTOL fighter-bombers.

On the forecastle, abreast the the SA-N-3 launcher and the 76mm mounting, are four pairs of elevating launchers for SS-N-12 anti-ship missiles, and it is thought that a further 16 reloads are carried below-decks between the two groups of launchers. The reloads are stowed on either side of a narrow lift which brings them up from the magazine. They are then lined up with the launchers via a system of rails.

The long, narrow hangar running from beneath the forward end of the flight deck to the stern accommodates two squadrons of helicopters and a squadron of Yak-36 Forger VTOL aircraft. Hangar and flight deck are served by two lifts, 62 x 33ft (19 x 10m) and 62 x 16.5ft (19 x 5m) respectively. The larger of the two is close to the centre-line amidships; the smaller is ▶

Right: An early view of *Kiev,* with four Hormone helicopters lined up on the flight deck and a single Yak-36 Forger aft.

Below: *Minsk,* the second ship of the class, underway in the Pacific Ocean.

117

▶ immediately aft of the island superstructure. There are several smaller lifts for deck tractors, personnel and munitions. The flight deck itself is angled at 4° and has seven small helicopter spots marked out, with a larger spot aft for Forger landings. The angled portion of the flight deck and the after deck-park are covered with heat-resistant tiles to absorb the thrust of the Forger's two vertical-lift engines.

Kiev was clearly designed from the outset to operate VTOL aircraft. The initial plans for the ship must date from the mid-1960s, when the experimental "Freehand" VTOL aircraft made a series of test flights which led to the development of the Forger. It was probably thought that these developments would enable the Kievs to put up VTOL interceptors against attacking aircraft, thus allowing them to operate in open-ocean areas such as the Norwegian Sea and the Pacific without land-based fighter cover. The Forger does not, however, appear to be a particularly successful aircraft. It lacks the speed and endurance for an effective interceptor, and its inability to make a rolling take-off imposes severe limitations on its payload. It is probably more successful in the ground support role and might also be employed for reconnaissance; for driving away enemy surveillance and ASW patrol aircraft; and for attacks on small ships.

Kiev is deployed to the Northern Fleet and *Minsk* to the Pacific Fleet. *Novorossisk* will probably join *Kiev* following sea trials. In the event of hostilities the Kievs would be employed in support of Soviet submarines in their respective areas against NATO surface and underwater threats. This would involve both defensive postures, to protect the SSBN bastions in the Barents Sea and the Sea of Okhotsk, and offensive forays, to sweep aside NATO barrier ASW forces in key areas such as the GIUK Gap. Operations of the latter type provide the main justification for the heavy battery of SSMs. The ability of the Kievs to perform such a mission is, however, heavily dependent on the deployment of NATO carrier battle groups, for the SS-N-3 is outranged by the strike aircraft carried by the US Navy's carriers.

Right: *Minsk* operating off the Philippines. Note the hinged doors in the centre of the stern for VDS (variable depth sonar). The large vertically ribbed door is thought to allow access to boats carrying bulky stores, and there is a small elevator above it at the after end of the flight deck. The other indentation has a stern refuelling point and vents for the refuse incineration plant.

Far right: An overhead view of *Minsk* with Hormones on the forward part of the flight deck and Forgers aft. The flight deck is covered with heat-resistant tiles.

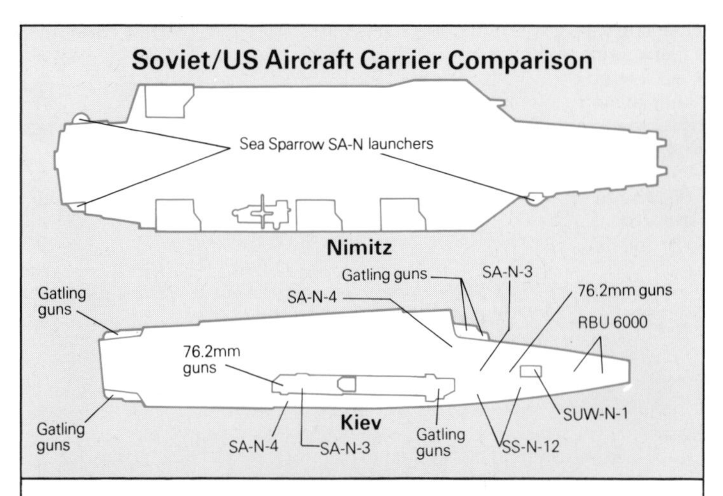

Above: These two plan views show clearly the basic differences in design philosophy between *Kiev* and a typical attack carrier of the US Navy. In the *Nimitz* aviation features are of primary importance, and only point-defence weapons are carried. *Kiev,* on the other hand, devotes far less space to her air complement but has a wide variety of weapon systems including long-range antiship missiles and missiles for area defence and ASW. The offensive capabilities of *Kiev* lie in her armament; those of *Nimitz* lie in her aircraft.

ASW CRUISER/PKR

Moskva

Completed: 1967-68, Nikolayev South.
Names: *Moskva, Leningrad.*
Displacement: 14,500t standard; 18,000t full load.
Dimensions: 625 oa x 112 x 25ft (191 x 34 x 8m).
Propulsion: 2-shaft geared steam turbines; 100,000shp = 30kt.
Armament: *ASW:* 18 Hormone A helicopters, twin SUW-N-1 launcher (20 ? missiles); two RBU 6000 mortars.
AAW: two twin SA-N-3 launchers (44 missiles); four 57mm (2x2).
Sensors: *Surveillance:* Top Sail, Head Net C.
Fire Control: two Head Lights, two Muff Cob.
Sonars: LF hull-mounted sonar, VDS.

When *Moskva* first appeared in 1967 she was the largest warship completed for the Soviet Navy since the Revolution. Designed to hunt US Navy SSBNs operating in the Eastern Mediterranean (which provided the best launch points against the Soviet Union during the early years of Polaris), *Moskva* was heavily influenced by the helicopter cruisers built for the French and Italian navies during the early 1960s.

Moskva is, however, a much larger vessel, able to accommodate an air group of 15-18 Hormone A antisubmarine helicopters in a capacious hangar beneath her half-length flight deck. The latter is served by two lifts, each 52 x 15ft (16 x 4.5m), and has a tractor garage at its forward end, set into the superstructure block with the flying control station above it. The narrow lifts have proved a problem when helicopters other than the Hormone have been carried: when Mi-8 Hip minesweeping helicopters were embarked by *Leningrad* in 1974 for the Suez clearance operation, they had to remain on deck.

The forward half of the ship is occupied by close- and medium-range antisubmarine weapons and a comprehensive suite of air defence systems. The massive block superstructure, which terminates in a tall pyramid-shaped uptake for the steam propulsion system, is built up in steps to accommodate the fire control and surveillance radars.

The missile launchers, positioned on the centre-line to give good arcs, also rise in steps. Closest to the bow is the SUW-N-1 launcher, which fires the nuclear-tipped FRAS-1 antisubmarine missile. Farther aft are the SA-N-3 launchers for surface-to-air missiles. Both the SUW-N-1 and SA-N-3, together with the Head Lights guidance radars and the large Top Sail 3-D ▶

Below: Profile view of the Moskva-class PKR; only two such vessels were completed.

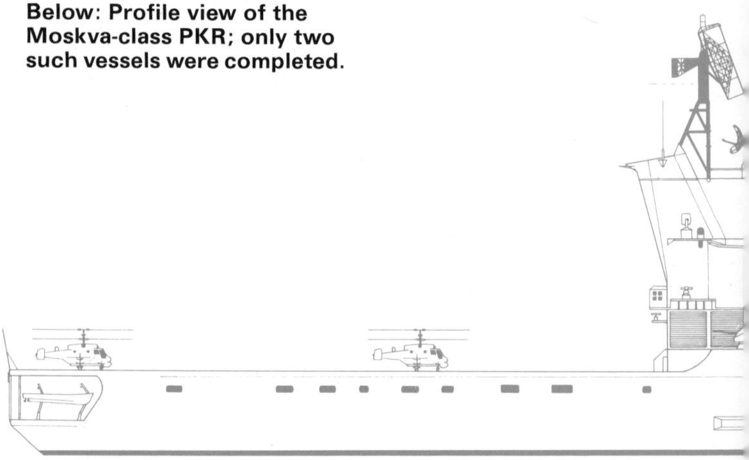

Above: The antisubmarine cruiser *Moskva* operating in the Mediterranean where land-based air cover is available.

Above: The stern of *Moskva,* showing the towing mechanism for the variable depth sonar located in a well beneath the flight deck overhang.

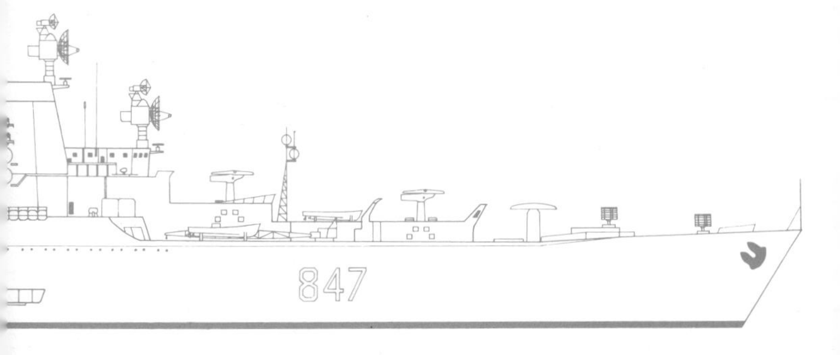

▶ surveillance radar associated with the SA-N-3, made their first appearance on *Moskva*. The SA-N-3 was to become the most important Soviet naval air defence system of the 1970s and was installed on every major warship class during that period.

Only two units of the Moskva class were completed. They have operated exclusively in the Black Sea and Mediterranean, with only an occasional sortie to take part in exercises in other Fleet Areas. The ships' lack of integral fighter defence was presumably acceptable for operations in the Eastern Mediterranean, given the proximity of friendly air bases, but it remains their major weakness. There is also evidence to suggest that *Moskva* and *Leningrad* have proved relatively ineffectual in their primary mission of hunting SSBNs, although their construction may well have influenced US Navy operating practices and have hastened the development of longer-range submarine-launched missiles.

Above: *Moskva* operating Hormone helicopters. The mesh mats covering the helo-circles are to prevent slippage in rough weather.

Left: *Moskva* underway in the Mediterranean in company with a BPK of the Kashin class.

Below: *Moskva* in the Mediterranean being overflown by a P-2 Neptune ASW aircraft of the US Navy.

LARGE ASW SHIP/BPK

Udaloy

Completed: 1981 onwards, Kaliningrad and Zhdanov Yard (Leningrad).
Names: *Udaloy, Vize-Admiral Sulakov* (+ 2 building).
Displacement: 7,000t standard; 8,500t full load.
Dimensions: 520 oa x 59 x 20ft (158 x 18 x 6m).
Propulsion: 2-shaft COGAG; 100,000bhp = 32kt.
Armament: *ASW:* two Hormone A helicopters; eight SS-N-14 missiles (2x4); two RBU 6000 mortars; ten 21in (533mm) TT (2x5) *AAW:* eight VLS canisters for SA-N-?; two 100mm (2x1), four 30mm gatlings.
Sensors: *Surveillance:* two Strut Pair.
Fire Control: two Eye Bowl, Kite Screech, two Bass Tilt (radar for SAMs not yet fitted).
Sonars: LF bow sonar, VDS.

The new Soviet BPK *Udaloy* bears a remarkable resemblance in both size and concept to the US Navy's *Spruance* class DDs. The similarities extend even to the layout of the gas-turbine propulsion machinery which, contrary

Below: Profile view of *Udaloy*. Vertical launch canisters are fitted on the forecastle and between the after funnel and double hangar.

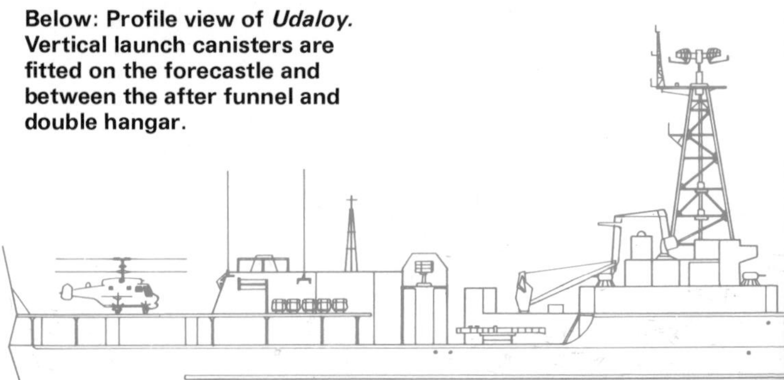

to recent Soviet practice, is arranged as two separate units.

The other noteworthy feature of the *Udaloy* is the increased specialization of the armament, in which ASW qualities have been maximised to the detriment of other capabilities. There are no anti-ship weapons; only a short/medium range SAM system comprising eight vertical launch canisters divided equally fore and aft is fitted, making fewer demands on ship space than the SA-N-3 system of earlier BPKs. The surveillance radars installed are lightweight, two-dimensional models with limited range.

ASW armament, on the other hand, is exceptionally powerful. As well as the now standard quadruple SS-N-14 launchers abreast the bridge and the RBU mortars and torpedo tubes amidships, *Udaloy* has two separate hangars side by side for Hormone A helicopters, giving onto a spacious landing platform above the stern. A large low-frequency sonar seems probable, and there is an independent variable depth sonar.

In view of the similarity in displacement and dimensions between *Udaloy* and *Sovremenny*, her anti-surface counterpart, it is somewhat surprising that there should be so little standardization as regards hull-form and propulsion system. The most likely explanation for this is the difference in weapon and sensor outfits, together with the tactical requirement for lower noise emission in ASW ships—hence the adoption of gas-turbines.

Above: *Udaloy* on sea trials. The armament is already aboard, but there are a number of empty platforms for electronic apparatus.

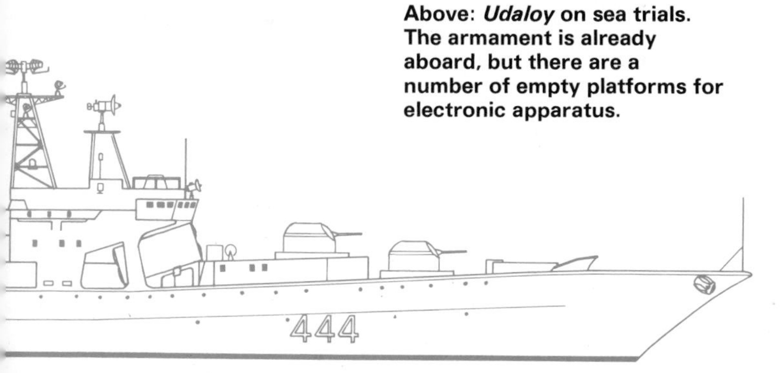

LARGE ASW SHIP/BPK

Kara

Completed; 1973-79, 61 Kommuna (Nikolayev).
Names: *Azov, Kerch, Nikolayev, Ochakov, Petropavlovsk, Tallin, Tashkent.*
Displacement: 8,200t standard; 9,500t full load.
Dimensions: 570 oa x 60 x 20ft (174 x 18 x 6m).
Propulsion: 2-shaft COGAG; 100,000bhp = 32kt.
Armament: *ASW:* eight SS-N-14 missiles (2x4); Hormone A helicopter; two RBU 6000 and two RBU 1000 mortars; ten 21in (533mm) TT (2x5).
AAW: two twin SA-N-3 launchers (44 missiles); two twin SA-N-4 launchers (36 missiles); four 76mm (2x2); four 30mm gatlings.
Sensors: *Surveillance:* Top Sail, Head Net C.
Fire Control: two Head Lights, two Pop Group, two Owl Screech, two Bass Tilt.
Sonars: LF bow sonar, VDS.

The Kara class was a development of the Kresta II BPK (see pages 36-39). Gas-turbine propulsion was adopted in place of steam, resulting in major modifications to the layout of the midships section. Uptakes for the four large aero-derived gas turbines were led up into a single square funnel and the Head Net C surveillance radar was shifted forward to a lattice mast atop an enlarged bridge structure to take it clear of the hot exhausts.

In the Kara class, a 50ft (15m) section was added between the bridge structure and the tower mast to accommodate a larger gun calibre and the new SA-N-4 close-range surface-to-air missile. The latter was mounted in cylindrical "bins" on either side of the tower mast, with the adjacent Pop Group guidance radars protected by high, curved blast screens. The close-in anti-missile gatlings were moved aft to a position abreast the funnel. One consequence of this arrangement is a "blind" arc of a full 50° aft and 20° forward for the SA-N-4 launchers—a defect shared with other side-mounted systems.

The only major modification to the sensor outfit was the installation of a variable depth sonar beneath the flight deck.

The size of the bridge structure in the Kara class—wider, a deck higher, and nearly twice as long as that of the Kresta II—indicates a significant increase in command and control spaces. There is, however, nothing in the way the Karas have been deployed to suggest that they are intended to serve as▶

Right: A Kara-class BPK exercising in the Mediterranean. The twin-arm SA-N-3 is in the reloading position and the ship's Ka-25 ASW helicopter is visible on the landing pad aft.

Below: Profile of the Kara-class BPK. The weapons systems and overall layout owe much to the Kresta II.

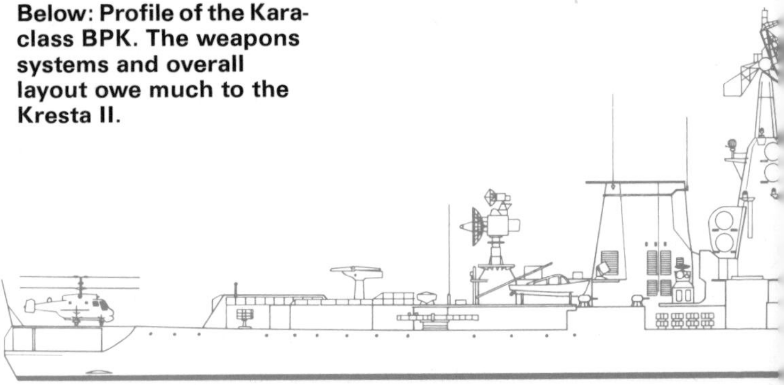

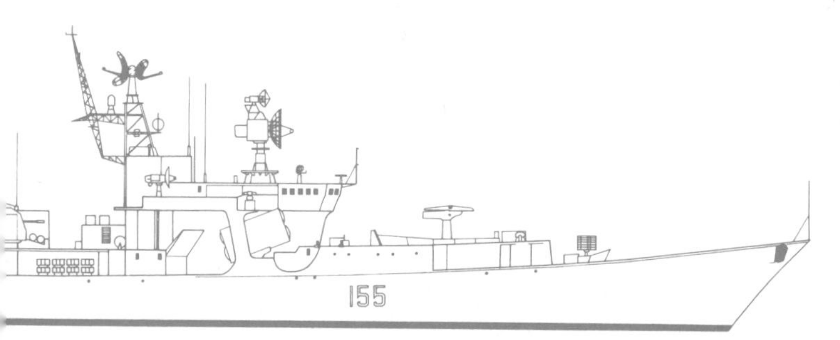
155

▶flagships for groups of other vessels. Two later units have been allocated to the Pacific Fleet, but the bulk of the class serves exclusively in the Black Sea and the Mediterranean. The significant enhancement of close-range AAW capability in the Karas—and their construction in Black Sea, not Baltic, shipyards—suggests that they were designed for service in this particular area.

Since her completion in 1977, *Azov* has served as trials ship for the new SA-N-6 vertical launch system and has remained in the Black Sea. The after SA-N-3 launcher and Head Lights radar were suppressed in favour of experimental installations. *Petropavlovsk* was completed without RBU 1000 launchers aft and is fitted instead with TACAN drums on platforms projecting from the sides of the hangar.

Production of the Kara class has recently been terminated in favour of a larger cruiser designated "BLACKCOM 1" by NATO. This ship is estimated at 12-14,000 tons and is thought to be fitted with long-range cruise missiles as well as anti-air and antisubmarine weapons.

Above: An aerial view of the forward part of a Kara-class BPK, showing clearly the quadruple launchers for SS-N-14 missiles.

Right: An early view of *Nikolayev,* with the side-mounted weapons well in evidence. Note the VDS housing in the stern.

Below: ***Nikolayev*** **in the Mediterranean.**

LARGE ASW SHIP/BPK

Kresta II

Completed: 1970-78, Zhdanov Yard (Leningrad).
Names: *Admiral Isachenkov, Admiral Isakov, Admiral Makarov, Admiral Nakhimov, Admiral Oktyabrsky, Admiral Yumashev, Kronshtadt, Marshal Timoshenko, Marshal Voroshilov, Vasily Chapaev.*
Displacement: 6,000t standard; 7,500t full load.
Dimensions: 520 oa x 56 x 20ft (158 x 17 x 6m).
Propulsion: 2-shaft geared steam turbines; 100,000shp = 34kt.
Armament: *ASW:* eight SS-N-14 missiles (2x4); Hormone A helicopter, two RBU 6000 and two RBU 1000 mortars; ten 21in (533mm) TT (2x5).
AAW: two twin SA-N-3 launchers (44 missiles); four 57mm (2x2); four 30mm gatlings.
Sensors: *Surveillance:* Top Sail, Head Net C.
Fire Control: two Head Lights, two Muff Cob, two Bass Tilt.
Sonars: MF bow sonar.

The Kresta II class ships were a result of the crash ASW building programme of the late 1960s. The design was a modification of the Kresta I Rocket Cruiser, with the anti-ship systems replaced by antisubmarine weapons.

In place of the SS-N-3 cruise missiles on each side of the bridge structure there are quadruple box launchers for SS-N-14 A/S missiles–the first installation of this system on a Soviet warship. The Hormone B missile guidance helicopter of the Kresta I was replaced by the A ASW version. A significant modification was made to the ship's handling arrangements, involving the construction of a platform deck above the low quarterdeck. The extra height thus gained must facilitate helicopter take-off and landing operations in a seaway, but the two-tier hangar arrangement, in which the hangar roof has to be raised to enable the helicopter to be positioned on a lift which then descends to become the hangar floor, is extraordinarily complex and awkward.

A new medium frequency bow sonar was fitted, resulting in a modified clipper bow with considerable overhang. Even this improvement in detection capabilities is, however, inadequate to exploit the full 25nm (45km) range of

Below: Profile and plan views of the Kresta II-class BPK. Note the massive Top Sail 3-D air search radar.

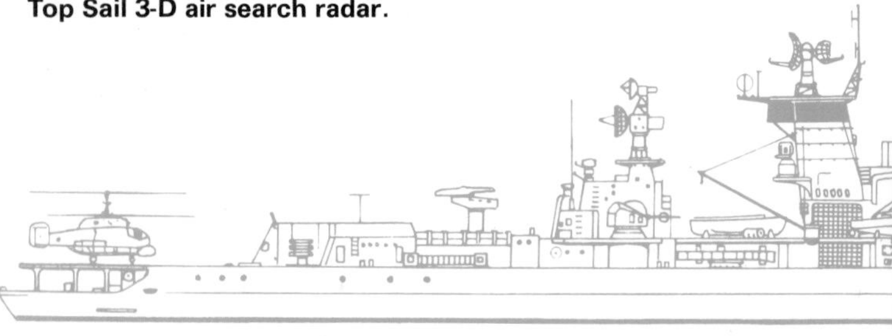

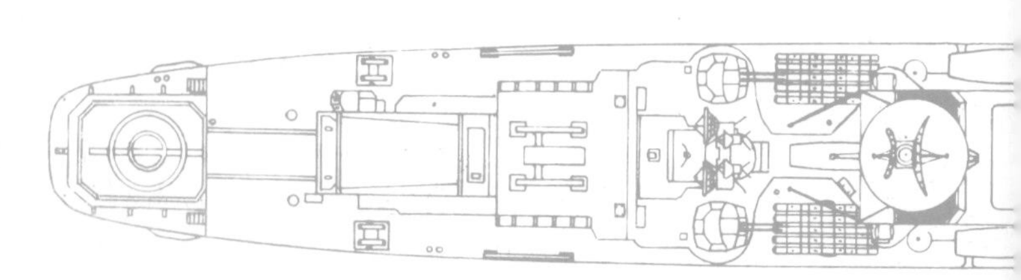

the SS-N-14, which can be guided in the mid-course phase using the fire control radars for the surface-to-air missiles. At longer ranges the ship would appear to rely on data from external sources, including its own helicopter—fitted with a dipping sonar—and other vessels in the hunting group.

The new SA-N-3 surface-to-air missile system, introduced three years earlier on the Moskva class cruisers, replaced the SA-N-1 system of the Kresta I. While the layout of the launchers and fire control radars remained the same, modifications had to be made to the central tower mast in order to compensate for the additional topweight involved in fitting the massive Top Sail 3-D radar.

In addition to the automatic twin 57mm mountings a new close-in anti- ▶

Above: A Kresta II operating on antisubmarine practice duties in the Mediterranean.

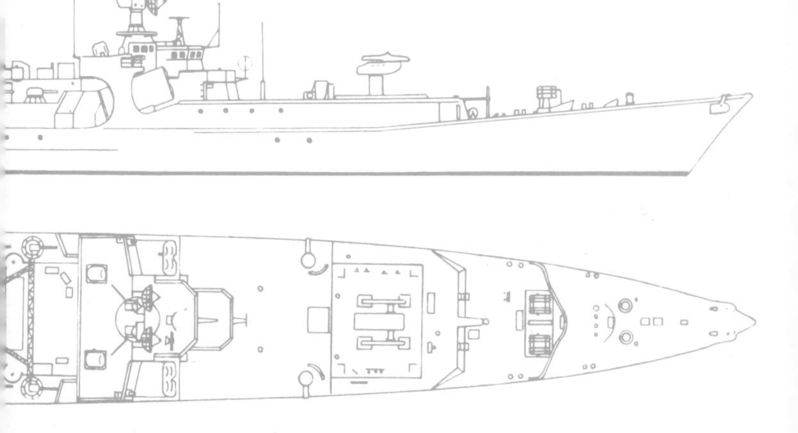

▶ missile system of four gatling guns, each with six rotating barrels, was fitted forward of the tower mast.

The Kresta II class continued in production at the rate of one per year until the late 1970s, construction proceeding in parallel with the Black Sea-built Kara class from 1972 onwards. The Soviets clearly regard the Kresta II as a successful design: even the limited number of A/S missiles carried–there is no reload system–does not appear to be considered a major disadvantage, for more recent classes show no increase in missile provision. The major

Above: *Admiral Makarov* underway in the Mediterranean. Note the hinged roof of the hangar.

Below: *Admiral Yumashev* operating in the North Atlantic, on her way to the naval base at Murmansk.

defect of the design is the lack of internal volume, resulting in a cramped ship with no margin for later modifications. The small, narrow, bridge structure has proved inadequate to accommodate the necessary command and control spaces, and later ships have had additional structures built up between the bridge and the central tower mast.

Most units of the class serve with the Northern Fleet and they have frequently operated in company with *Kiev* on depoyments. The other units serve with the Pacific Fleet.

Above: A Kamov Ka-25 Hormone A helicopter on the landing pad of a Kresta II-class BPK.

LARGE ASW SHIP/BPK

Kanin

Completed: 1961-62, Zhdanov Yard (Leningrad), Nikolayev; Komsomolsk.
Names: *Boiky, Derzky, Gnevny, Gordy, Gremyashchy, Uporny, Zhguchy, Zorky.*
Displacement: 3,700t standard; 4,700t full load.
Dimensions: 456 oa x 48 x 16ft (139 x 15 x 5m).
Propulsion: 2-shaft geared steam turbines; 84,000 shp = 34kt.
Armament: *ASW:* three RBU 6000 mortars; ten 21in (533mm) TT (2x5).
AAW: twin SA-N-1 launcher (22 missiles); eight 57mm (2x4); eight 30mm (4x2).
Sensors: *Surveillance:* Head Net C.
Fire Control: one Peel Group, one Hawk Screech, two Drum Tilt.
Sonars: MF bow-mounted sonar.

These eight ships were originally Rocket Ships of the Krupny class, armed with SS-N-1 launchers for Scrubber anti-ship missiles fore and aft and four quadruple 57mm AA mountings. When the SS-N-1 became obsolescent in the mid-1960s, it was decided to convert the vessels as ASW ships on a similar pattern to the Kotlin SAM. The conversions were undertaken at the Zhdanov Yard, Leningrad, and later at Komsomolsk in the Pacific, from 1968 to 1977.

An SA-N-1 launcher was installed aft atop its own magazine and a tower for the Peel Group guidance radar was constructed forward of the second funnel. Only two 57mm mountings were retained forward. Whereas little modification had been made to ASW capabilities in the Kotlin conversion (*see* **Kotlin SAM**), the Kanin had a new medium-frequency bow sonar installed and three MBU 6000 mortars fitted, two of them abreast the tower mast and the third on the forecastle. The twin banks of torpedo tubes were expanded from triple to quintuple mountings. The bridge was enlarged and the electronics updated. A helicopter platform was fitted aft, but no maintenance facilities were provided. All the Kanins now have four twin 30mm mountings abreast the second funnel and Drum Tilt FC radars installed on platforms projecting from the radar tower.

The Kanin class appears to be a much more successful conversion than the smaller Kotlin SAM, and has far superior ASW qualities, although the weapons themselves are somewhat dated by modern standards. Most ships of the class serve either with the Northern or the Pacific Fleets.

Below: Profile and plan views of the Kanin-class BPK.

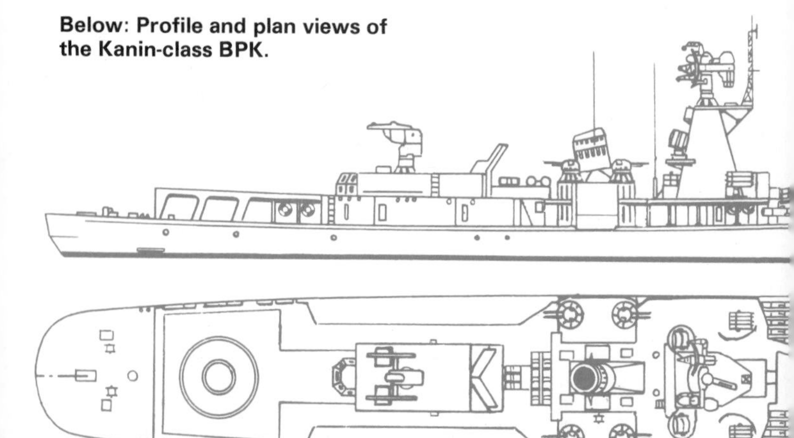

Above: An early Kanin conversion prior to installation of the 30mm Gatlings and Bass Tilt fire control directors.

Above: A BPK of the Kanin class shadowing HMS *Hermes* during NATO exercises in Northern waters in October 1973.

LARAGE ASW SHIP/BPK

Kashin

Completed: 1962-70, Zhdanov Yard (Leningrad); 61 Kommuna Yard (Nikolayev).
Names: *Komsomolets Ukrainy, Krasny-Kavkaz, Krasny-Krim Obraztsovy, Odarenny, Provorny, Reshitelny, Skory, Smetlivy, Soobrazitelny, Sposobny, Steregushchy, Strogy, Stroiny.*
Displacement: 3,750t standard; 4,500t full load.
Dimensions: 471 oa x 53 x 15ft (143 x 16 x 5m).
Propulsion: 2-shaft COGAG; 96,000bhp = 35kt.
Armament: *AAW:* two twin SA-N-1 launchers (44 missiles); four 76mm (2x2).
ASW: two RBU 6000 and two RBU 1000 mortars; five 21in (533mm) TT (1x5).
Sensors: *Surveillance:* two Head Net A *or* Big Net and Head Net C.
Fire Control: two Peel Group, two Owl Screech.
Sonars: HF bow/hull-mounted (?) sonar.

The Kashin class were built as large multi-purpose destroyers with good AAW and ASW capabilites. Their primary mission as originally conceived may have been to provide additional protection to Kynda class cruisers in their anti-carrier role. The Kashins, however, proved more successful in service than the Kyndas, and continued in series production in both the Baltic and the Black Sea throughout the 1960s. ▶

Below: A profile view of the Kashin-class BPK. Later units have Big Net and Head Net C in place of the twin Head Net A antennae.

Above: Bow shot of a Kashin-class BPK; the SA-N-1 launcher is particularly evident in this view.

Left: A Kashin-class BPK at anchor in the Mediterranean.

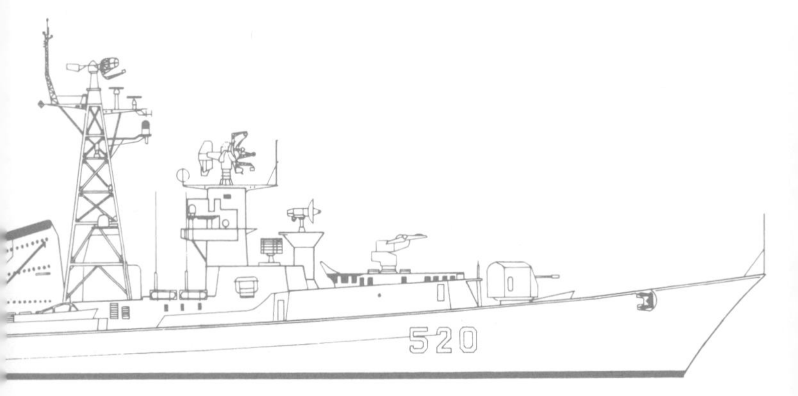

▶ The most remarkable technological achievement of the design lay in its all-gas-turbine propulsion plant. Although a number of NATO navies were already experimenting with gas-turbines in hybrid combinations, the installed horsepower of the Kashin remained unmatched in the West until the completion of the light aircraft carrier HMS *Invincible* in 1980. Four large industrial gas-turbines, each of about 24,000shp, were installed, the uptakes being led up into distinctive paired funnels angled outboard to keep the hot gases clear of the radars. Following sea trials, the forward pair of funnels had to be heightened.

The Kashins were the first Soviet ships with a "double-ended" SAM system. An unusual feature of the launchers is that they reload while trained to port and starboard respectively, suggesting a modular launcher/magazine installation. Early ships carried two single Head Net A air search radars atop the two lattice masts; but ships completed in the mid/late 1960s had the second antenna replaced by the longer-range Big Net aerial, and the first by a back-to-back Head Net C.

The ASW armament comprises antisubmarine mortars fore and aft and torpedo tubes amidships. It was originally thought that the sonar fitted was hull-mounted, but it has recently been suggested that it may be a small bow sonar. Some Kashins have a helicopter landing spot marked out on the fantail, but in others of the class this has been painted over. There are no facilities for helicopter maintenance.

From 1971 onward some ships of the Kashin class were converted as Rocket Ships (*see* **Kashin-Mod.**). *Provorny* has recently been fitted out as a trials ship for the new SA-N-7 medium-range surface-to-air missile: both SA-N-1 launchers and their Peel Group guidance radars have been removed. The photographs available (of poor quality, and not reproduced here) show a single-arm launcher aft and a Top Steer 3-D radar atop a new mainmast. The forward Peel Group radar has been replaced by a Head Net C.

Successful in their time, the Kashins have provided the Soviet Navy with invaluable operating experience, especially with regard to their novel propulsion system. They serve in all four Soviet fleets, with the majority in the Black Sea or the Pacific. They have, however, undergone no modernization and must therefore be considered obsolescent.

Above: *Strogy* of the Soviet Pacific Fleet at Massawa (Ethiopia) in the early 1970s. Note the Big Net air search radar atop the mainmast; this was an improvement on the earlier Head Net A.

Below: A Kashin operating with the Soviet Mediterranean Squadron—they serve with all four Soviet fleets.

PATROL SHIP/SKR

Krivak I/II

Completed:	1971 onward, Zhdanov Yard (Leningrad); Kamysch-Burun (Kerch), Kaliningrad.
Names Krivak I:	*Bditelny, Bezzavetny, Bodry, Buzukoriznenny, Deyatelny, Doblestny, Dostoiny, Druzhny, Leningradsky Komsomolets, Letuchky, Pylky, Razumny, Razyashchy, Retivy, Silny, Storozhevoi, Svirepy, Zadorny, Zharki.*
Krivak II:	*Bessmenny, Gordelivy, Gromky, Grozyashchy, Neukrotimy, Razytelny, Rezky, Rezvy, Ryany* (+ 1).
Displacement:	3,300t standard; 3,600t full load.
Dimensions:	405 oa x 46 x 16ft (123 x 14 x 5m).
Propulsion:	2-shaft COGAG; 50,000bhp = 30kt.
Armament:	*ASW:* Four SS-N-14 missiles (1x4); two RBU 6000 mortars; eight 21in (533mm) TT (2x4). *AAW:* two twin SA-N-4 launchers (36 missiles); four 76mm (2x2, Krivak I) *or* two 100mm (2x1, Krivak II).
Sensors:	*Surveillance:* Head Net C. *Fire Control:* two Eye Bowl, two Pop Group, one Owl Screech. *Sonars:* MF bow sonar, VDS.

The Krivak was designed as a "2nd-rate" counterpart to the "1st-rate" Kresta II and Kara classes, with which it initially shared the same BPK classification. Although the class followed on from the Kashin in terms of construction dates, it was in no sense a successor to the Kashin class. The Krivak is smaller, has an altogether more sophisticated ASW outfit, lacks an area defence SAM system–arguably the main armament of the Kashin–and is easier to build. The latter factor made it possible to allocate construction to the smaller Baltic and Black Sea shipyards, leaving the slipways of the traditional naval yards free for the construction of larger units.

The major ASW system is the SS-N-14 missile, fired from a bulky quadruple launcher forward, This is backed up by RBU 6000 mortars immediately forward of the bridge and torpedo tubes amidships. The bow sonar is probably the same model as that fitted in the Kresta II and the Kanin conversions; there is, in addition, an independent variable depth sonar on the stern.

Only close-range air defence is provided, in the form of SA-N-4 "bins" fore and aft and a pair of 76mm mountings (later ships, designated Krivak II, have single 100mm). The Krivak is almost unique in its generation in having no "last-ditch" anti-missile system such as the 30mm gatling. ECM provision is also minimal compared with the "1st-rate" BPKs.

The propulsion system is a simple gas-turbine plant. The small size of the funnel suggests that there are only two turbines, almost certainly the same model installed in the contemporary Kara. If this is so, it seems likely that the

Below: Profile of a Krivak I. The Krivak II has single 100mm mountings in place of the twin 76mm of the first group.

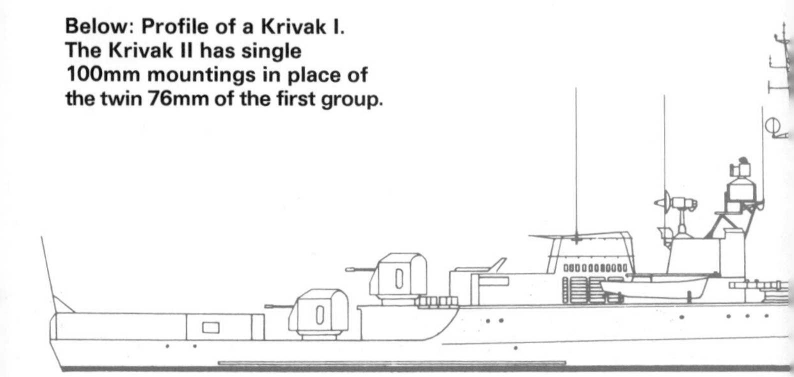

Above: Overhead view of a Krivak I showing the distinctive square funnel and the prominent VDS housing aft.

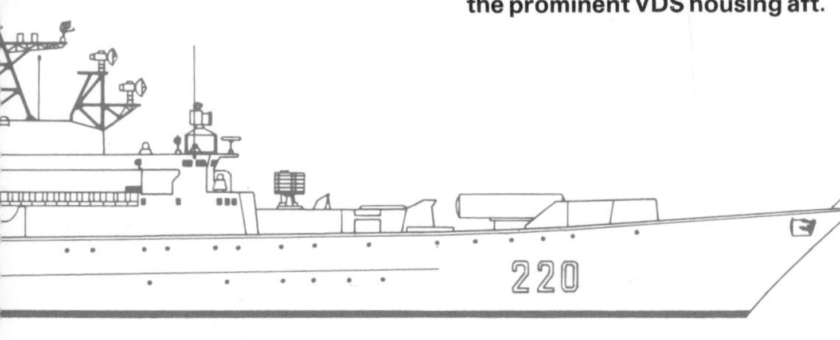

turbines are located side-by-side in a single engine-room, making for an exceptionally compact propulsion plant but increasing vulnerability to damage. The high rating of the turbines must also result in heavy fuel consumption at cruising speed.

The Krivak has never been the heavily-armed super-destroyer that Western commentators have claimed, nor was it designed as such. The complement of antisubmarine missiles is small by Western standards, and there is no shipborne helicopter to provide target data and independent ASW at longer ranges; AAW and ECM capability is inadequate for open-ocean operations; and the propulsion system, while easy to maintain, probably leaves the Krivaks short on endurance. They are, nevertheless, clearly adequate for their intended mission, for production has continued at a rate of three to four ships per year over the past twelve years and shows no sign of coming to an end.

Above: A Krivak I in the English Channel. The quadruple SS-N-14 launcher forward houses antisubmarine missiles.

One in every three Krivaks has been allocated to the Baltic, where the class has become the major ASW unit. The remaining Krivaks have been used to supplement the larger BPKs and ASW cruisers in the other three fleets. In 1977-78 their classification was changed to SKR, suggesting that as the new 8,000-ton BPKs become available in greater numbers the Krivaks may altogether relinquish their open-ocean role in favour of the defence of the SSBN bastions.

Below: An overhead view of a Krivak I, giving an excellent view of the layout. The RBU 6000 mortars can be seen forward of the bridge, with the torpedo tubes amidships.

ROCKET CRUISER/RKR(?)

Kirov

Completed: 1980 onward, Baltisky Yard (Leningrad).
Names: *Kirov* (?) (+ 1 building).
Displacement: 23,100t full load.
Dimensions: 814 oa x 75 x 25ft (248 x 23 x 8m).
Propulsion: 2-shaft CONAS; 120,000shp = 30kt.
Armament: *SSM:* twenty SS-N-19 missiles with two (?) Hormone B missile guidance helicopters.
AAW: twelve hatches for SA-N-6 missiles (72? missiles); two SA-N-4 launchers (36 missiles); two 100mm (2x1); eight 30mm gatlings.
ASW: twin SS-N-14 launcher (16? missiles); three (?) Hormone A helicopters; one RBU 6000 and two RBU 1000 mortars; ten 21in (533mm) TT (2x5).
Sensors: *Surveillance:* Top Pair, Top Steer.
Fire Control: two Top Globe, two Pop Group, two Eye Bowl, one Kite Screech, four Bass Tilt.
Sonars: LF bow sonar, VDS.

Kirov is the ultimate realization of the Soviet Rocket Cruiser concept. Her powerful defensive armament and extensive command facilities enable her to perform her primary mission of challenging NATO surface forces either alone or at the centre of a Surface Action Group. The need for such capabilities, in addition to a large battery of anti-ship missiles, has resulted in a ship more than twice the displacement of any Western cruiser currently in service.

Below: A profile view of the Rocket Cruiser *Kirov.* Note the bare forecastle which houses the vertical launch systems.

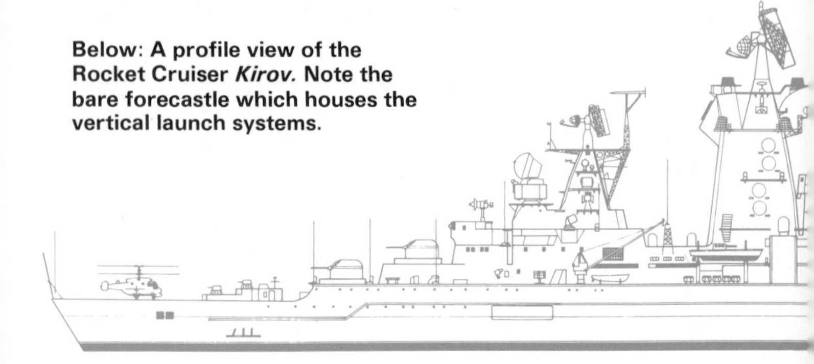

Above: *Kirov* underway. The spacious helicopter landing pad has the lift and hangar forward of it between the after Gatlings. *Kirov* is thought to operate both A and B variants of the Kamov Ka-25 helicopter.

Left: *Kirov* photographed by a US Navy aircraft. She is capable of a maximum speed of more than 30kt.

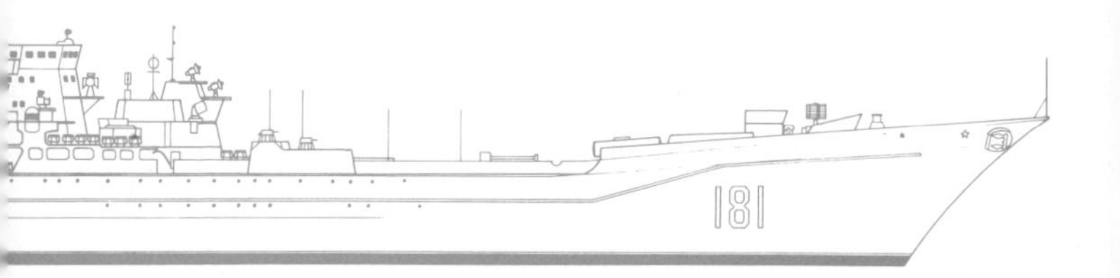

▶ The main armament comprises twenty SS-N-19 anti-ship missiles, with a range of about 250nm (460km). These are housed in an extensive box magazine, 66ft x 40ft (20m x 15m) and perhaps 33ft (10m) deep, just forward of the main superstructures, and are fired vertically from individual silos, each covered by a hinged hatch. The magazine itself may well be armoured. The vertical launch system, which dispenses with reloads, enables saturation missile attacks to be launched against a high-value target such as a Carrier Battle Group.

Forward of the SS-N-19 magazine is the major surface-to-air system, which also employs vertical launch. There are twelve hinged hatches, arranged in three rows of four. The asymmetrical disposition of the three rows suggests a reloading mechanism sited between them with a magazine beneath, possibly for some 60 reloads. The SA-N-6 is thought to be a high-performance missile with a range of at least 27nm (50km) and a speed of Mach 5 to 6. Since the large Top Globe guidance radars are at either end of the ship, it seems likely that an autopilot is employed in the initial phase of flight, the missile being subsequently picked up by the guidance radar and deposited close enough to the target for its homing head to take over. Whatever the exact nature of the guidance system, it would be surprising, in view of the adoption of vertical launch, if a number of missiles could not be kept in the air simultaneously.

The SA-N-6 system is backed up by launchers for the close-range SA-N-4 abreast the forward deckhouse; two single-mounted 100mm guns aft; and four groups of 30mm gatlings in the "quadrants" of the ship. ECM are also exceptionally complete.

Tucked inside the break in the forecastle is a twin-tube launcher for SS-N-14 antisubmarine missiles. Target data are provided by a large low-frequency bow sonar–probably the same model as on *Kiev*–and an independent variable depth sonar. In addition to the customary mortars and torpedo tubes–the latter behind sliding doors in the hull–there are probably▶

Left: A bow view of *Kirov.* The cable which runs along the hull may be for degaussing. The Top Pair air surveillance and tracking radar is visible atop the central mack with small Palm Frond navigation and surface surveillance radars just below it on platforms.

Below: *Kirov* is pictured here on her way to join the Soviet Northern Fleet. The massive central structure is crowded with electronics which include satellite communications aerials and an extensive ECM/ESM outfit.

Above: This overhead view of *Kirov* shows clearly the two sets of hatches for SS-N-19 and SA-N-6 vertical launch missiles.

▶three Hormone A helicopters for longer-range antisubmarine search and attack and to assist with targeting for the SS-N-14 missiles. The Hormone As, and possibly a further two helicopters of the Hormone B missile guidance version, are accommodated in a hangar beneath the quarterdeck. A 40ft x 16ft (15m x 5m) lift at the forward end of the quarterdeck descends to form part of the hangar floor, the opening being closed by twin hinged doors. This arrangement increases stowage space in the hangar.

The propulsion system of *Kirov* is thought to be a Combined Nuclear and Steam (CONAS) plant. Two nuclear reactors, each rated at about 35,000shp, give a cruising speed of 24kt (44km/h), while the steam plant–either in the form of independent geared turbines or of oil-fired superheaters–provides the necessary boost to give a maximum speed of more than 30kt (56km/h). This seems an unduly complex arrangement; it was probably made necessary by the limited power available from proven Soviet marine reactors.

Kirov is clearly a very powerful ship indeed and incorporates a number of significant technological advances, including the first operational vertical launch system in the world. If she has a weakness it is that she represents such a considerable investment of resources that she constitutes a high-value target on a par with the carriers she is designed to hunt. This may impose restrictions on her deployment in the event of hostilities.

Right: A stern view of *Kirov* showing the single 100mm mountings above the helicopter landing pad. The large door set into the stern conceals the towing mechanism for a big VDS.

ROCKET CRUISER/RKR

Kresta I

Completed: 1967-70, Zhdanov Yard (Leningrad).
Names: *Admiral Zozulya, Sevastopol, Vize-Admiral Drozd, Vladivostok.*
Displacement: 6,140t standard; 7,500t full load.
Dimensions: 510 oa x 56 x 20ft (156 x 17 x 6m).
Propulsion: 2-shaft geared steam turbines; 100,000shp = 34kt.
Armament: *SSM:* four SS-N-3 launchers (2x2) with Hormone B missile guidance helicopter.
AAW: two twin SA-N-1 launchers (44 missiles); four 57mm (2x2); four 30mm gatlings (*Drozd* only).
ASW: two RBU 1000 and two RBU 6000 mortars; ten 21in (533mm) TT (2x5).
Sensors: *Surveillance:* Big Net, Head Net C.
Fire Control: one Scoop Pair, two Peel Group, two Muff Cob, two Bass Tilt (*Drozd* only).
Sonars: HF hull-mounted sonar.

The Kresta I class cruiser was the successor to the Kynda. It incorporated a number of important modifications, partly as a result of problems experienced with the Kyndas in service, but also because of a shift in emphasis towards open-ocean operations, necessitating changes in the armament balance.

Only two twin launchers for the SS-N-3 anti-ship missile were fitted. No reloads were carried, and the excessive topweight of the Kyndas was further reduced by the adoption of a single tower mast. The unit machinery arrangement of the Kyndas was abandoned in favour of a more compact steam plant, with the uptakes trunked together side by side in a single funnel.

The increasing importance assigned to air defence was evidenced by the doubling of the surface-to-air missile armament, the two twin SA-N-1 launchers occupying the key centre-line positions fore and aft. The distinctive Side Globe broad-band ECM jammers, of which four are fitted on either side of the central tower, made their first appearance on this class. Detection was enhanced by the installation of a Big Net long-range air surveillance radar.

One Hormone B missile guidance helicopter is carried, giving the Kresta I an integral capability for targeting and mid-course guidance beyond horizon range. The helicopter is operated from the low quarterdeck; this must cause problems in severe weather conditions.

Although the Kresta Is have only limited ASW capabilities, the ships when completed were given the same BPK designation as the Kresta II class modification. They have recently been reclassified RKR. *Vladivostok* serves with the Pacific Fleet and the remaining three with the Northern Fleet.

Below: Profile of a Kresta I-class RKR. *Vize-Admiral Drozd* has paired Gatlings between the bridge structure and the central tower, and Bass Tilt FC radars in the bridge wings.

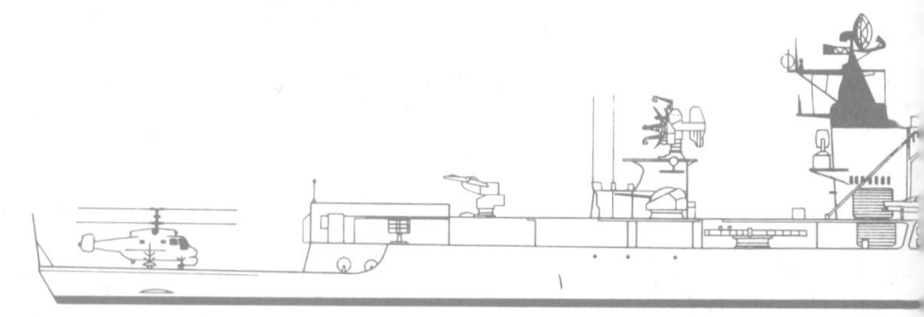

Above: *Vize-Admiral Drozd* in the Caribbean in 1970. Following a visit to Cuba she took part in the first OKEAN exercise.

Above: Another view of *Vize-Admiral Drozd* in the Caribbean. Note the change in pennant number—a common occurrence with warships of the Soviet Navy.

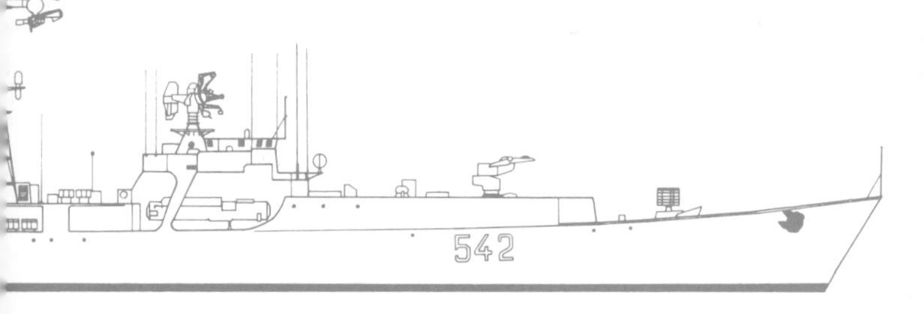

ROCKET CRUISER/RKR

Kynda

Completed: 1962-65, Zhdanov Yard (Leningrad).
Names: *Admiral Fokin, Admiral Golovko, Grozny, Varyag.*
Displacement: 4,400t standard; 5,700t full load.
Dimensions: 466 oa x 52 x 17ft (142 x 16 x 5m).
Propulsion: 2-shaft geared steam turbines; 100,000shp = 34kt.
Armament: *SSM:* eight SS-N-3 launchers (2x4, 16 missiles).
AAW: twin SA-N-1 launcher (22 missiles); four 76mm (2x2).
ASW: two RBU 6000 mortars; six 21in (533mm) TT (2x3).
Sensors: *Surveillance:* two Head Net A *or* one Head Net C, one Head Net A.
Fire Control: two Scoop Pair, one Peel Group, one Owl Screech.
Sonars: HF hull-mounted sonar.

The Kynda was the Soviet Navy's first purpose-built missile ship, the Krupny and Kildin classes which preceded it being modifications of conventional destroyer designs. A new, distinctive hull-form with a long forecastle, a low quarterdeck and a square cut-away stern was adopted, setting a pattern for later missile cruisers. The Kynda was given a modern block superstructure and two tall, enclosed tower masts to carry air surveillance radars and the guidance radars for the anti-ship missiles.

The SS-N-3 missiles are fired from massive quadruple launchers fore and aft; eight reloads are carried inboard of the launchers in the forward and after superstructures respectively. Because the Kyndas were designed to operate in conjunction with land-based aircraft and submarines in the defence of Soviet sea-space, they rely on an external source for targeting and mid-course guidance beyond horizon range.

Above: The Rocket Cruiser *Admiral Golovko* in the Mediterranean.

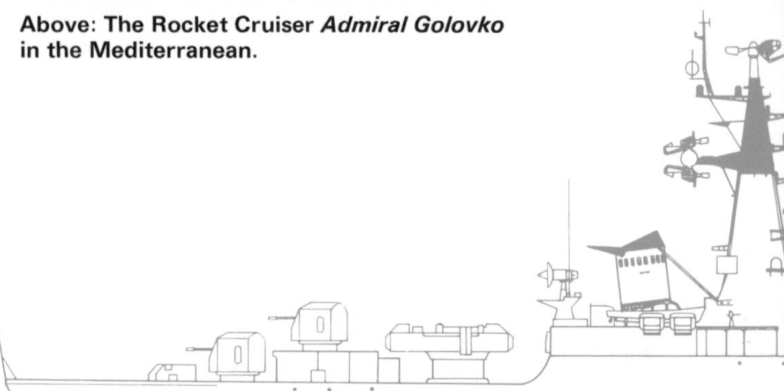

Above: *Grozny*, the other Black Sea-based ship of the class. Her ECM outfit distinguishes her from her sisters.

AAW and ASW was accorded less importance than in later designs, and it may be that additional protection was to be provided by the Kashin-class destroyers.

The major defect of the Kynda design was excessive topweight, which brought with it stability problems and resulted in the abandonment of construction beyond four units in favour of a larger and more seaworthy design, the Kresta I. Of the four ships completed, two serve with the Black Sea Fleet and two in the Pacific.

Below: Profile of the Kynda-class RKR.

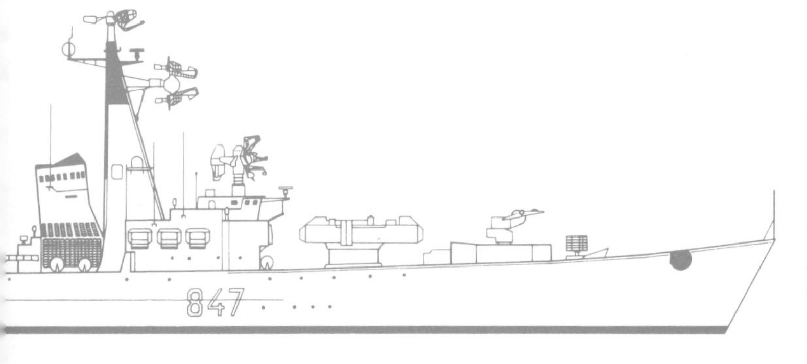

LARGE ROCKET SHIP/BRK

Sovremenny

Completed: 1980 onward, Zhdanov Yard (Leningrad).
Names: *Sovremenny* (+ 3 building).
Displacement: 6,500t standard; 7,950t full load.
Dimensions: 510 oa x 57 x 20ft (155 x 17 x 6m).
Propulsion: 2-shaft geared steam turbines; 100,000shp = 33kt.
Armament (conjectural): *SSM:* six SS-N-9 missiles (2x3) with Hormone B guidance helicopter.
Fire Support: two 180mm (2x1).
AAW: Single SA-N-7 launcher; four 30mm gatlings.
ASW: two RBU 1000 mortars; four 21in (533mm) TT (2x2).
Sensors: *Surveillance:* Top Steer.
Fire Control: Band Stand, Kite Screech, two Bass Tilt, six unidentified.
Sonars: MF bow sonar.

In 1980 the first of a new series of destroyers with a clear anti-surface mission made its appearance in the Baltic. *Sovremenny* ran her sea-trials without her main armament but with most of her surveillance and fire control radars in place.

Below: Profile view of *Sovremenny*. The major calibre gun mountings have now been installed but not the antiship missiles.

The Band Stand FC radar suggests that the anti-ship missile, for which there are spaces on either side of the bridge structure, will be the SS-N-9. Immediately aft of the funnel is a telescopic hangar for a Hormone B missile guidance helicopter. Major calibre guns of a new model have now been installed fore and aft; the single mountings appear to be 180mm guns–the calibre adopted for the pre-war Kirov-class cruisers–presumably intended for fire support operations. The gun bears a remarkable similarity to the 8in (203mm) gun under development for the US Navy during the late 1970s.

The other major weapon system, still to be fitted, is a medium-range surface-to-air system for which space has been reserved between the bridge and the forward gun mounting. It will almost certainly be the single-launcher SA-N-7 which has been undergoing trials aboard the Kashin-class destroyer *Provorny*.

ASW armament is minimal, comprising only a pair of RBU mortars and twin banks of torpedo tubes. There is a bow sonar, but no variable depth sonar.

It is somewhat surprising that the Soviet Navy should have persisted with steam propulsion in this class, especially as its ASW counterpart, the *Udaloy* is powered by gas-turbines.

Below: *Sovremenny* on sea trials in the Baltic. Her main armament has yet to be installed, although the sensor outfit appears to be almost complete.

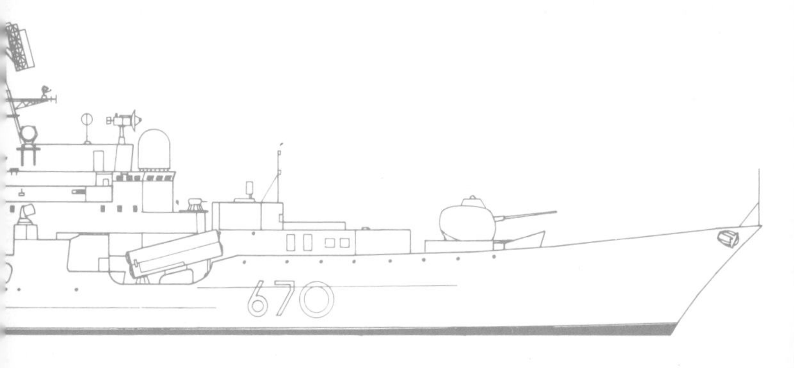

Kashin-Mod

Completed: 1963-72, Zhdanov Yard (Leningrad); 61 Kommuna Yard (Nikolayev).
Names: *Ognevoy, Sderzhanny, Slavny, Smely, Smyshlenny.*
Displacement: 3,950t standard; 4,950t full load.
Dimensions: 481 oa x 53 x 16ft (147 x 16 x 5m).
Propulsion: 2-shaft COGAG; 96,000bhp = 35kt.
Armament: *SSM:* four SS-N-2C (4x1).
AAW: two twin SA-N-1 launchers (44 missiles); four 76mm (2x2); four 30mm gatlings.
ASW: two RBU 6000 mortars; five 21in (533mm) TT (1x5).
Sensors: *Surveillance:* two Head Net A *or* Big Net and Head Net C.
Fire Control: two Peel Group, two Owl Screech, two Bass Tilt.
Sonars: HF bow/hull-mounted sonar, VDS.

Beginning in 1971, six ships of the Kashin class, including one unit then still under construction, were taken in hand for conversion as Rocket Ships. Four SS-N-2C horizon-range anti-ship missiles were fitted abreast the after superstructure. Variable depth sonar was installed on a remodelled stern, increasing overall length by about 10ft (3m), and a helicopter platform was built above it. The after pair of RBU 1000 antisubmarine mortars was removed and replaced by a new deckhouse on which were mounted four 30mm gatlings together with their Bass Tilt directors. No significant modifications were made to the major AAW weapon systems or to the sensor outfit.

A number of these conversions were undertaken in Black Sea shipyards. The units thus modified were subsequently deployed as "shadows" for the

Above: A Kashin-Mod. in company with a carrier of the US 6th Fleet in the Mediterranean. Note the helicopter pad added to the remodelled stern.

Below: A profile view of the Kashin-Mod. class BRK.

carriers of the US Navy Sixth Fleet, with the apparent intention of making a preemptive strike, using the aft-firing SS-N-2C missiles, and extricating the ship as quickly as possible in the event of an outbreak of hostilities.

It was at first thought that the entire Kashin class would be similarly modified: but the conversion may not have been a complete success. Topweight may be a problem, for a considerable amount of new equipment was installed for the loss of only two small A/S mortars. It also seems illogical to have installed a new VDS while halving the already minimal antisubmarine armament; this was a classic illustration of the Soviet tendency to add on whatever new items of equipment happen to be available without considering the ship as a total weapon system.

One of the first ships converted, *Otvazhny*, was lost during sea trials in the Black Sea in 1974, apparently as the result of an internal explosion.

Above: A Large Rocket Ship of the Kashin-Mod. class underway. The door in the stern is for the VDS.

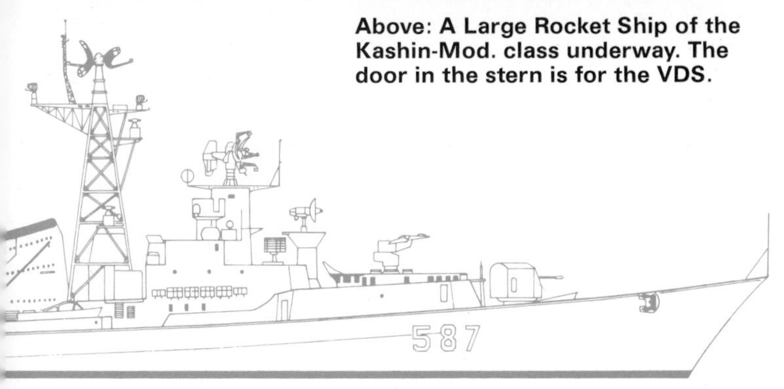

LARAGE ROCKET SHIP/BRK

Kildin

Completed: 1958, Nikolayev; Zhdanov Yard (Leningrad).
Names: *Bedovy, Neuderzhimy, Neulovimy, Prozorlivy.*
Displacement: 3,100t standard; 4,150t full load.
Dimensions: 418 oa x 42 x 16ft (128 x 13 x 5m).
Propulsion: 2-shaft geared steam turbines; 72,000shp = 35kt.
Armament (as modified): *SSM:* four SS-N-2C (4x1).
AAW: four 76mm (2x2); sixteen 57mm (*Bedovy* 45mm) (4x4).
ASW: two RBU 6000 mortars; four 21in (533mm) TT (2x2).
Sensors: *Surveillance:* Head Net C (*Bedovy,* Strut Pair).
Fire Control: one Owl Screech, one Hawk Screech.
Sonars: HF hull-mounted sonar.

As originally completed, the four Kildin class ships were missile conversions of the conventional Kotlin class destroyer. A single bulky launcher for the

Above; A Kildin-class ship after conversion; the bulky SS-N-1 launcher has been replaced by two twin 76mm mountings.

SS-N-1 Scrubber anti-ship missile was fitted aft, together with a large magazine. The remaining armament comprised two quadruple 57mm mountings forward of the bridge, a further two 57mm mountings abreast the mainmast, twin torpedo tubes amidships, and antisubmarine mortars close to the bow.

By the late 1960s the SS-N-1 was obsolescent and was already being removed from the Krupny class, which underwent an ASW conversion. It was then decided to take in hand three of the Kildin class ships in order to update them. The SS-N-1 launcher was removed and replaced by two twin 76mm mountings, and an Owl Screech FC director was installed atop the short lattice mainmast. Anti-ship capability was restored, however, by fitting four cylindrical launchers for the SS-N-2C horizon-range missile abreast the after structure. The main surveillance radar was also updated.

The conversions were undertaken by Black Sea yards from 1971 onward and the modified ships have since been deployed to the Mediterranean Squadron, where they have been employed together with similarly modified Kashins to shadow carriers of the American Sixth Fleet. The Pacific Fleet unit. *Neuderzhimy,* retains her original configuration as is illustrated by the photograph at the foot of this page.

Below: An unmodified Rocket Ship of the Kildin class at anchor in the Mediterranean Sea.

COMMAND SHIP/KRU

Sverdlov-Mod

Completed: 1954-57, Nosenko Yard (Nikolayev); Komsomolsk.
Names: *Zhdanov, Admiral Senyavin.*
Displacement: 16,000t standard; 17,500t full load.
Dimensions: 689 oa x 72 x 25ft (210 x 22 x 8m).
Propulsion: 2-shaft geared steam turbines; 110,000shp = 30kt.
Armament: *Zhdanov:* nine 152mm (3x3); twelve 100mm (6x2); thirty-two 37mm (16x2); eight 30mm (4x2); twin SA-N-4 launcher (18 missiles).
Admiral Senyavin: six 152mm (2x3); twelve 100mm (6x2); thirty-two 37mm (16x2); sixteen 30mm (8x2); twin SA-N-4 launcher (18 missiles); two helicopters.
Sensors: *Surveillance:* Top Trough.
Fire Control: one Long Ears, two Sun Visor, one Pop Group, two Drum Tilt (four in *Senyavin*)

In 1970 two of the ageing Sverdlov class cruisers were taken in hand at Nikolayev and modified as specialized Command Ships.

Zhdanov, emerging in 1973, had her third 152mm turret replaced by a tall deckhouse, probably housing a new signals department. A tall tripod mast with lattice supports carrying Veecone HF antennae was constructed forward of the new deckhouse. An SA-N-4 missile "bin" was installed in the top of the deckhouse, with its Pop Group guidance radar on a platform projecting from the new tripod mainmast. Four twin 30mm mountings together with their Drum Tilt radars were fitted around the fore-funnel. The mine-rails on the quarterdeck were replaced by a helicopter landing circle.

The conversion of *Admiral Senyavin* (completed in 1974) was even more extensive. Both after 152mm turrets were replaced by a hangar for two Hormone helicopters. In addition to the 30mm fitted around the funnel, four more mountings were installed atop the hangar, with paired Drum Tilt radars on twin pedestals at its after end. The rest of the modifications were identical to those of *Zhdanov.*

Above: The command cruiser *Zhdanov* in the Mediterranean.

Since completing their respective conversions these two cruisers have served as flagships of two of the four Soviet fleets: *Zhdanov* is based in the Black Sea and *Admiral Senyavin* in the Pacific.

Below: An overhead view of *Zhdanov.* Note the SA-N-4 "bin" atop the new after superstructure.

CRUISER/KR

Sverdlov

Completed: 1952-56. Baltiisky Yard (Leningrad); 402 Severodvinsk; Nosenko Yard (Nikolayev); Komsomolsk.
Names: *Admiral Lazarev, Admiral Ushakov, Aleksandr Nevsky, Aleksandr Suvorov, Dmitri Pozharsky, Dzerzhinsky, Mikhail Kutusov, Murmansk, Oktyabrskaya Revolutsiya, Sverdlov.*
Displacement: 16,000t standard; 17,500t full load.
Dimensions: 689 oa x 72 x 25ft (210 x 22 x 8m).
Propulsion: 2-shaft geared steam turbines; 110,000shp = 30kt.
Armament: Twelve 152mm (4x3); twelve 100mm (6x2); sixteen 37mm (8x2); sixteen 30mm (8x2; *Okt. Rev.* only). *Dzerzhinsky:* twin SA-N-2 launcher; nine 152mm (3x3); twelve 100mm (6x2); eight 37mm (4x2).
Sensors: *Surveillance:* Big Net *or* Top Trough, Knife Rest (some ships).
Fire Control: two Long Ears, two Sun Visor, four Drum Tilt (*Okt. Rev.* only).
Dzerzhinsky: Surveillance: Big Net.
Fire Control: Fan Song E, one Long Ears, two Sun Visor.

The Sverdlov was to have been the major surface unit in the Soviet post-war surface navy. Twentyfour ships were planned but construction came to an abrupt halt when Nikita Khrushchev assumed power and promptly declared the naval programme out-dated. Only fourteen units were completed.

The *Sverdlov* is a traditional cruiser design incorporating the results of war experience and follows on from the Chapaev. One ship was transferred to Indonesia in 1962 and a further unit decommissioned in 1969, but most remain in service with the Soviet Navy. They appear to be retained partly for training purposes, but also to provide much-needed command facilities. As that need diminishes, it is to be expected that further ships will be discarded. Another justification for the Sverdlovs' retention is that they are the only remaining Soviet ships capable of gunfire support operations; but this too is a requirement which will be met in the future by new construction, such as the Sovremenny class.

In 1960 *Dzerzhinsky* was taken in hand for conversion to the SA-N-2 surface-to-air missile system, which replaced the third 152mm mounting and some of the smaller AA guns. The conversion was unsuccessful, apparently because the SA-N-2 proved difficult to gather after launch, and the conversion was not extended to the remainder of the class. Two further ships were converted as Command Ships in the early 1970s (*see* **Sverdlov-Mod.**).

Above: The cruiser *Aleksandr Suvorov* underway in the Philippine Sea during OKEAN exercises.

Below: The missile cruiser *Dzerzhinsky* in the Mediterranean. The conversion was apparently unsuccessful.

DESTROYER/EM

Kotlin Sam

Completed: 1954-57, Leningrad, Nikolayev, Komsomolsk.
Names: *Bravy, Nakhodchivy, Nastoychivy, Nesokrushimy, Skromny, Skrytny, Soznatelny, Vozbuzhdenny.*
Displacement: 2,850t standard, 3,600t full load.
Dimensions: 418 oa x 42 x 15ft (128 x 13 x 4.5m).
Propulsion: 2-shaft geared steam turbines, 72,000shp = 36kt.
Armament: *AAW:* twin SA-N-1 launcher (22 missiles), two 130mm (1x2), four 45mm (*Bravy,* 12) (1/3x4), eight 30mm (three ships only).
ASW: two RBU 6000; five 21in (533mm) TT (1x5).
Sensors: *Surveillance:* Head Net C (*Bravy,* Head Net A).
Fire Control: one Peel Group, one Sun Visor, one Hawk Screech, two Drum Tilt (ships with 30mm only)
Sonars: HF hull-mounted sonar.

In 1962 the first missile conversion of a Kotlin class destroyer was completed. The ship chosen, *Bravy,* served as an experimental prototype for two years beore further conversions were undertaken.

The principal modification was the installation of a twin SA-N-1 launcher atop its own magazine in place of the after 130mm and 45mm mountings. A prominent pyramid-shaped tower carrying the Peel Group missile guidance radar replaced the former small lattice mainmast. A new after funnel was

Above: A destroyer of the Kotlin SAM II group. The pyramid-shaped tower carrying the Peel Group radar is a distinctive feature.

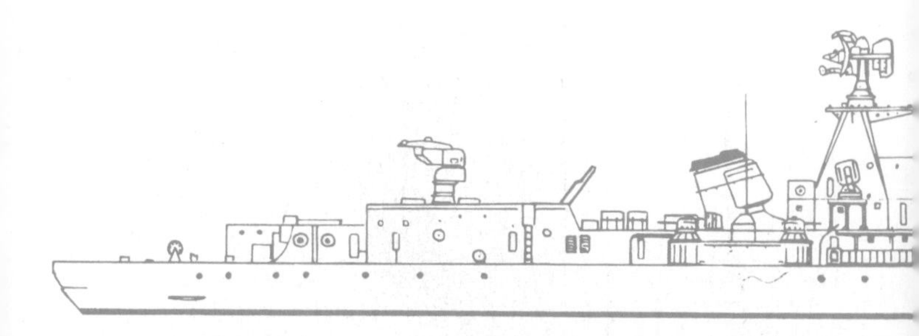

designed to double as a blast deflector for the missiles. Initially, the midships 45mm mountings and the torpedo tubes were removed, but they were restored in 1964.

Seven further units (plus one for Poland) were converted between 1966 and 1972. The original Kotlin funnel was retained in these ships and the radar tower differed in shape from that of *Bravy*. The midships 45mm were again discarded, although the last three units converted were fitted with four twin 30mm mountings in their place, together with Drum Tilt FC directors. The original 16-barrel, hand-loaded, antisubmarine mortars were replaced by automatic RBU 6000s. The air surveillance radar was updated.

Topweight problems may have been a factor in the decision to convert only eight units of the Kotlin class. Although deployed to all four Soviet fleets, the majority of the Kotlin SAMs serve with the Black Sea and Pacific Fleets.

Below: A destroyer of the Kotlin SAM II type with her forward guns elevated. The SA-N-1 launcher is also prominent on top of its magazine.

Below: A profile view of a Kotlin SAM II.

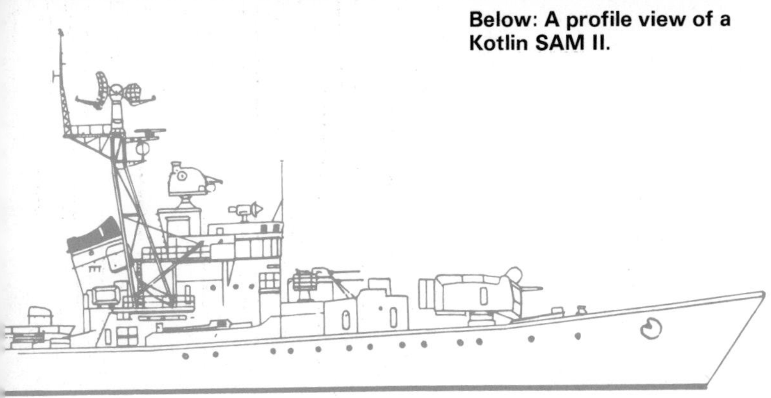

DESTROYER/EM

Kotlin

Completed: 1954-57, Leningrad, Nikolayev, Komsomolsk.
Names: *Blagorodny, Blestyashchy, Burlivy, Byvaly, Dalnevostochny Komsomolets, Moskovsky Komsomolets, Naporisty, Plamenny, Speshny, Spokoiny, Svedushchy, Svetly, Vdokhnovenny, Vesky, Vliyatelny, Vozmushchenny, Vyderzhanny, Vyzyvayushchy.*
Displacement: 2,850t standard; 3,800t full load.
Dimensions: 418 oa x 42 x 15ft (128 x 13 x 5m).
Propulsion: 2-shaft geared steam turbines; 72,000shp = 36kt.
Armament: *AAW:* four 130mm (2x2); sixteen 45mm (4x4); four to eight 25mm (2/4x2) (some ships only).
ASW: two RBU 2500 *or* RBU 6000; two RBU 600 (some ships only); five to ten 21in (533mm) TT (1/2x5).
Sensors: *Surveillance:* Slim Net.
Fire Control: Sun Visor, two Hawk Screech.
Sonars: HF hull-mounted.

The Kotlin class were the last conventional destroyers built for the Soviet Navy. Similar in layout to the earlier Skory class, the Kotlin incorporated a number of new technical developments, including stabilised turrets for the dual-purpose 130mm guns and a new quadruple 45mm mounting. The result was a powerful, seaworthy design–but one which was already outdated by the time the first unit was completed. The construction programme was therefore terminated in favour of new designs, armed with antiship missiles.

From 1962 onward, nine units of the class were converted to carry surface-to-air missiles (*see* **Kotlin SAM**). Eleven more units underwent a modification programme aimed at improving their ASW capability. RBU 2500 mortars were installed on either side of the forward 45mm mounting and the after bank of torpedo tubes was landed to compensate. Later conversions also had a pair of six-barrelled RBU 600 mortars on the stern, while some ships had the automatic RBU 6000 in place of the hand-loaded RBU 2500. Other modifications included the fitting of two or four twin 25mm mountings during the 1970s, and the experimental installation of helicopter platforms on three vessels.

A number of Kotlins have now decommissioned. Those that remain in service are probably used for training. Their only military value lies in their heavy gun armament, which would still be of use in fire support operations.

Above: A Kotlin-class destroyer underway in the Pacific. These were the final conventional destroyers to be built for the Soviet Navy.

Above: An unmodified destroyer of the Kotlin class underway. Although obsolescent the Kotlins have given good service and are still frequently to be observed on Soviet exercises and foreign deployment.

Left: An overhead view of an unmodified Kotlin. Note the two banks of quintuple torpedo tubes still in place.

DESTROYER/EM

Skory

Completed: 1952-55, Leningrad; Nikolayev; Severodvinsk (?); Komsomolsk.
Names: *Bezuprechny, Bezukoriznenny, Ognenny, Ostorozny, Otvetstvenny, Ozhestochenny, Ozhivlenny, Serdity, Smotryashchy, Sokrushitelny, Solidny, Sovershenny, Statny, Stepenny, Stoyky, Stremitelny, Surovy, Svobodny, Vdumchivy, Vedushchy, Verny, Vnimatelny, Vrazumitelny* (+ 12).
Displacement: 2,240t standard; 3,100t full load.
Dimensions: 395 oa x 39 x 15ft (121 x 12 x 4.5m).
Propulsion: 2-shaft geared steam turbines; 60,000shp = 33kt.
Armament: *Unmodified ships:* four 130mm (2x2); two 85mm (1x2); eight 37mm (4x2); four 25mm (2x2) (some ships only); ten 21in (533mm) TT (2x5).
Modified ships: four 130mm (2x2); five 57mm (5x1); two RBU 2500; five 21in (533mm) TT (1x5).
Sensors: *Surveillance:* Slim Net (Mod.).
Fire Control: Hawk Screech (Mod.), Top Bow (others).

The Skory was the first Soviet post-war destroyer design. Based on the war-time Otlichny class, the Skory reflected traditional Soviet interests: a heavy torpedo armament was fitted and mine-rails ran from the forecastle break to the stern, but ASW armament was minimal.

The first ships had single 37mm AA guns on either side of the bridge and atop the after deckhouse; these were replaced by twin 37mm mountings on later units. Some ships had twin 25mm added abreast the after funnel during the 1970s.

By the late 1950s the Skorys were already obsolescent, and from 1958 to 1961 a number of units were refitted with a view to improving AAW and ASW capabilities. The forward bank of torpedo tubes was landed and replaced by a deckhouse; the entire light AA armament was suppressed and

Below: Profile and plan views of a Skory-class destroyer. The mine-rails can be clearly seen in the top view.

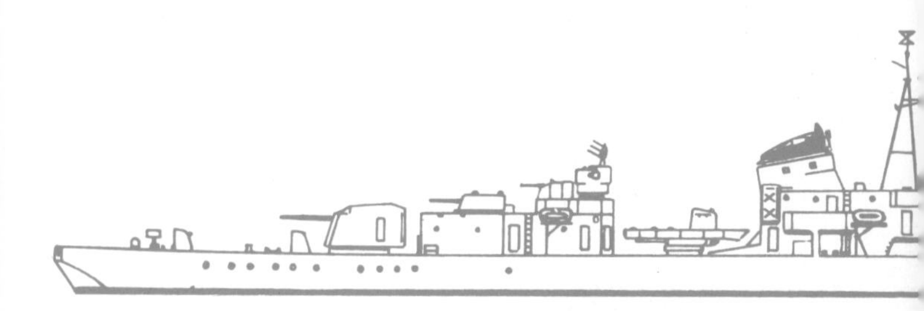

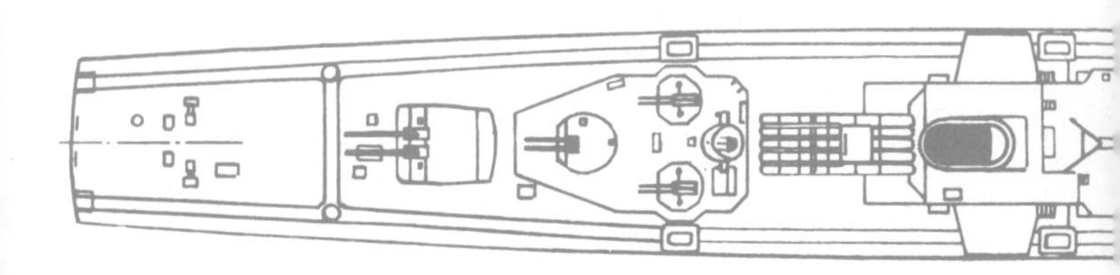

Above: An unmodified unit of the Skory class underway in the Mediterranean.

replaced by five single 57mm guns controlled by Hawk Screech FC directors; a new tripod mainmast with lattice supports, carrying a Slim Net air search radar, was fitted; and RBU 2500 antisubmarine mortars were installed forward of the bridge. The funnel cowlings were raised, giving the modified ships a distinctive appearance.

A number of destroyers of the Skory class were transferred to friendly or allied countries during the 1960s. Those which remained in service with the Soviet Navy received no significant modernization. The few in service today are mainly used for training.

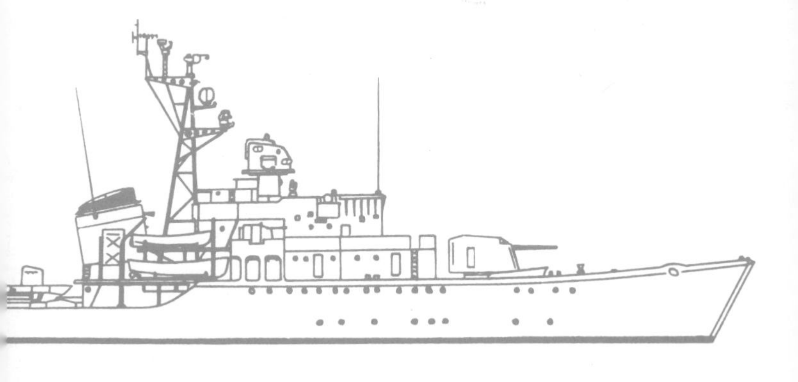

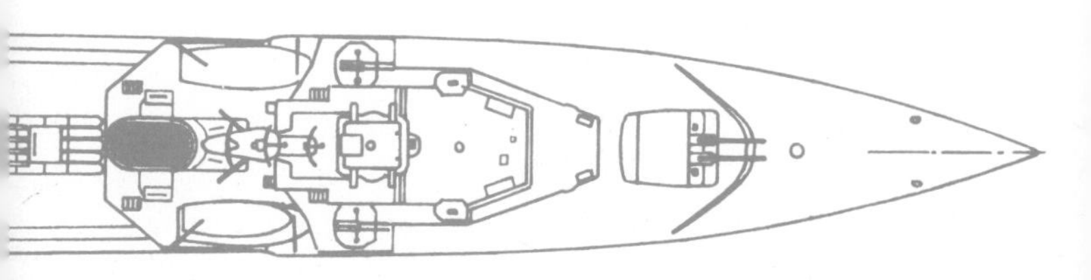

Coastal and Area Defence Vessels

The Soviet Navy's concept of area defence is an extension of Soviet Army philosophy. While the role of the ocean-going vessels is to contest control of the sea in open waters, area defence involves establishing total domination over the immediate operating areas of the respective fleets.

The basic components of the naval forces assigned to this particular task are: first, large missile boats, for defence of the periphery; second, patrol ships and antisubmarine vessels to establish control over the surface and sub-surface within these areas and to protect friendly maritime traffic (including amphibious forces); third, fast, mobile flotillas of missile- and torpedo-boats for a multitude of offensive and defensive tasks.

Most of the types in the second and third categories are capable of minelaying in addition to their primary mission.

The Soviet Navy will employ a traditional "layered" defence strategy to protect its own sea-space, with the naval forces supported by — and, indeed, heavily dependent on—a large land-based air force to provide air strike, fighter cover, reconnaissance, and missile relay, and to assist in ASW detection. For this reason, all surface units are fitted only with short-range anti-air weapons, and some ships which carry ASW weapons are not fitted with sonar.

Soviet classifications at this level are a downward

Above: An SKR (Storozhevoy Korabl') of the Mirka II class.

continuation of the categories outlined in the introduction to OCEAN-GOING SHIPS (pages 16-19), but with much more emphasis on the Patrol Ship category and with the addition of the Torpedo-Boat at the lowest level. In terms of size they are differentiated by the terms Ship, Small Ship, and Cutter *(Kater)*. The full list of designations is as follows:

Maly Protivolodochny Korabl' (MPK), Small Antisubmarine Ship; *Storozhevoy Korabl'* (SKR), Patrol Ship; *Maly Raketny Korabl'* (MRK), Small Rocket Ship; *Raketny Kater* (RKA), Missile-Boat; *Torpedny Kater* (TKA), Torpedo-Boat.

Below: An SKR of the Petya I class.

SMALL ASW SHIP/MPK

Pauk

Completed: 1980 onward.
No. in class: 1 +.
Displacement: 500t.
Dimensions: 205 oa x 26 x 10ft (63 x 8 x 3m).
Propulsion: 2-shaft diesels; ?bhp = 30kt.
Armament: *ASW:* two RBU 1200 mortars; four 15.7in (400mm) TT (4x1).
AAW: One 76mm; one 30mm gatling; SA-N-5 launcher.
Sensors: *Surveillance:* Strut Curve.
Fire Control: Bass Tilt.
Sonars: HF hull-mounted (?), VDS.

The first unit of the Pauk class appeared in 1980. The class is almost certainly a replacement for the ageing Poti: the hull-design, propulsion machinery and general layout are strikingly different, but the balance of the armament remains basically the same.

The Pauk has a slightly larger hull than the Poti, and a prominent knuckle and higher freeboard aft suggest that the Pauk will be a more seaworthy vessel than its predecessor. The superstructure comprises a single continuous

deckhouse topped amidships by the bridge. The propulsion system, unlike that of the Poti, is all-diesel, and because the exhaust vents are located in the side of the hull there is not the same competition for deck-space that existed in earlier gas-turbine-powered MPKs. A tall lattice mast carries the air surveillance radar and ESM antennae,. Projecting about 3ft (1m) beyond the stern is a prominent housing for a dipping sonar.

The ASW armament is still centred on a pair of mortars, located on either side of the forward superstructure, and four single 15.7in (400mm) torpedo tubes. The trend towards a heavier-calibre gun in recent small Soviet warships is also a feature of the Pauk, which has a single 76mm mounting on the forecastle. This is positioned well clear of the bridge, giving it far superior training arcs to the midships 57mm mounting of the Poti. For close-in anti-air defence there is an SA-N-5 launcher on the stern, backed up by a single 30mm gatling. Both the 76mm and the gatling are controlled by a single Bass Tilt director, mounted atop a prominent pedestal at the after end of the bridge structure.

The Pauk is a good design of its type and will undoubtedly enter series production for the Soviet Navy.

Below: An MPK of the Pauk class photographed in the Baltic. Note the new-design single 76mm mounting forward and the prominent VDS housing aft.

SMALL ASW SHIP/MPK

Grisha I/III

Completed: 1969 onward, Black Sea.
No. in class: 16 Grisha I; 20 Grisha III.
Displacement: 900t standard; 1,000t full load.
Dimensions: 237 oa x 33 x 11ft (73 x 10 x 3.5m).
Propulsion: 3-shaft CODAG; 22,000bhp = 32kt.
Armament: *ASW:* two RBU 6000; four 21in (533mm) TT (2x2).
AAW: twin SA-N-4 launcher (18 missiles); two 57mm (1x2); one 30mm gatling (Grisha III only).
Sensors: *Surveillance:* Strut Curve.
Fire Control: Pop Group, Muff Cob (I) *or* Bass Tilt (III).
Sonars: HF hull-mounted.

The Grisha appears to be a follow-on to the Poti class. Although in displacement it approaches the size of the Petya and Mirka, the Grisha has a hull-form which is clearly that of a vessel intended for coastal operations: freeboard aft is minimal, while the hull rises sharply towards the bow for good performance at higher speeds.

The layout of the propulsion machinery, which, as on the Poti, is a CODAG

Below: A Grisha I underway. Note the "bin" for SA-N-4 missiles forward of bridge, and the associated Pop Group guidance radar above the bridge. The antisubmarine mortars are mounted aft of the SA-N-4 launcher bin. The twin 57mm gun mounting aft is fully automatic, and has a high rate of fire. The KGB-operated Grisha IIs have a second 57mm gun.

installation, is conventional, with the gas-turbine uptake faired into a low funnel amidships and the diesel exhausts venting through the hull close to the waterline. The single gas-turbine is probably the same model as installed in the Petya and Mirka.

As in the Poti, the antisubmarine mortars are forward and the twin 57mm aft. Trainable twin tubes for 21in (533mm) torpedoes have replaced the fixed tubes for short antisubmarine torpedoes. The increase in size is largely accounted for by the installation of an SA-N-4 missile system on the forecastle, together with a Pop Group guidance radar above the bridge. A later variant, the Grisha III (1975 onward), also has a 30mm gatling aft, the original Drum Tilt radar being replaced by a Bass Tilt which controls both the 57mm and the 30mm mountings.

Construction of the Grisha proceeded at the rate of three ships per year throughout the 1970s. In addition to those ships serving with the Soviet Navy, six units are operated by the KGB. These have a second 57mm mounting in place of the SA-N-4 launcher.

Below: An MPK of the Grisha III class. This group can be distinguished from the earlier ships by the 30mm Gatling and Bass Tilt radar atop the after deckhouse. Another variant, the Grisha II, is in service with the KGB.

Poti

Completed: 1964-68, various yards.
No. in class: 64.
Displacement: 500t standard; 580t full load.
Dimensions: 196 oa x 26 x 9ft (60 x 8 x 3m).
Propulsion: 2-shaft CODOG; 24,000bhp = 34kt.
Armament: *ASW:* two RBU 6000 mortars; four 15.7in (400mm) TT (4x1).
AAW: two 57mm (1x2).
Sensors: *Surveillance:* Strut Curve.
Fire Control: Muff Cob.
Sonars: HF hull-mounted.

The Poti appeared at about the same time as the Mirka. Although both were originally classified MPK, the Mirka was larger and had a much heavier gun armament, justifying its later redesignation as an SKR. The Poti, on the other hand, was exclusively for ASW.

The most striking parallel between the Poti and the Mirka lies in the layout of the CODOG propulsion system. In both classes, the gas-turbines are installed in a raised stern section with identical prominent air intakes above it and openings in the stern for the exhaust gases. The diesels, used for cruising, are amidships with exhaust vents in the hull.

There are two superfiring RBU 6000 mortars forward and a twin 57mm mounting amidships. A number of the earlier vessels were completed with the older open mounting, but most ships have the automatic model. Four single 15.7in (400mm) antisubmarine torpedo tubes are angled out, two on either side of the gun mounting.

The Poti class was built in large numbers during the mid/late-1960s, until succeeded by the larger Grisha, with its improved anti-air capabilities. Although dated, the Poti remains the backbone of the Soviet coastal ASW forces.

Below: Profile and plan views of the Poti-class MPK. The angled antisubmarine torpedo tubes can be clearly seen in the top view.

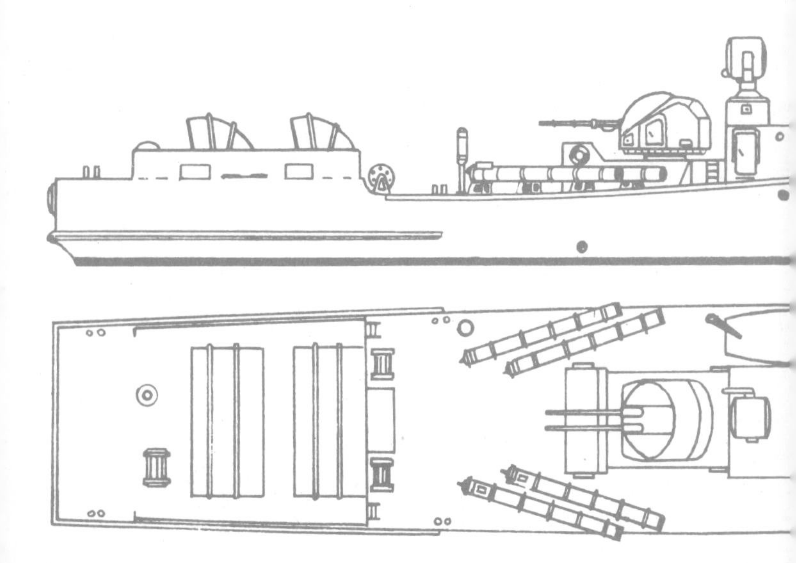

Above: A stern view of a Poti. Note the large 57mm mounting visible amidships, and the distinctive flaps in the stern for the twin gas-turbine exhausts.

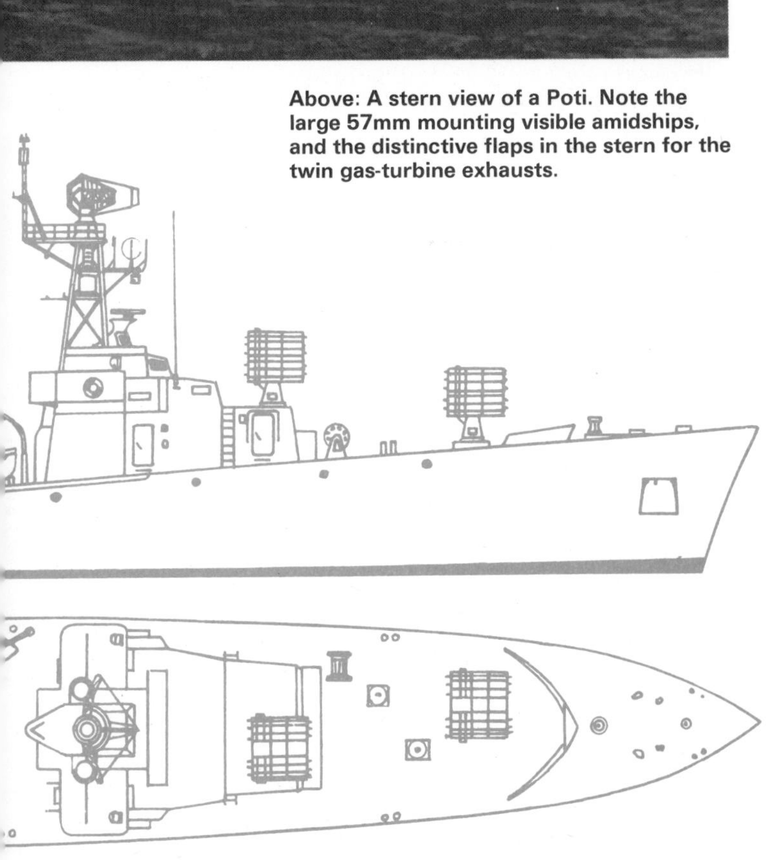

SMALL ASW SHIP/MPK

SO I

Completed: 1958-64, various yards.
No. in class: 45.
Displacement: 170t standard; 215t full load.
Dimensions: 138 oa x 20 x 6ft (42 x 6 x 2m).
Propulsion: 3-shaft diesels, 7,500bhp = 28kt.
Armament: *ASW:* four RBU 1200 mortars; two 15.7in (400mm) TT (2x1) (later boats only).
AAW: two to four 25mm (1/2x2).
Sensors: *Surveillance:* Pot Head.

Built as a successor to the Kronstadt class of the first postwar programme, the SO I class was heavily influenced by the SC-497 sub-chasers acquired from the USA under Lend-Lease. Intended primarily for the defence of harbour approaches, the SO I conforms to traditional Soviet practice in that it is fitted with mine-rails as well as the usual antisubmarine weapons. There are also degaussing cables along the sides of the hull, forward and amidships.

Four RBU 1200 mortars are grouped together on the forecastle, enabling these vessels to put down a carpet of depth bombs on forward bearings, and there are depth charge racks above the stern. The last ten units completed had their ASW capabilities boosted by the installation of two fixed tubes for homing torpedoes, the tubes being angled out on a forward bearing. In compensation, the after 25mm AA mounting was landed and the size of the depth charge racks reduced.

Between 150 and 200 SO I boats were completed, many being subsequently transferred to friendly or allied countries. They have the reputation of being poor sea-boats, and the proximity to the bow of the antisubmarine mortars must create maintenance problems.

Above: A subchaser of the SO I class at speed in the Baltic. The diesel exhaust is venting through the sides of the hull.

Below: The RBU 1200 mortars which comprise the main armament of the SO I are hand-loaded.

PATROL SHIP/SKR

Koni

Completed: 1977 onward, Black Sea.
Names: *Timofey Ol'yantsev* (+ 1?).
Displacement: 1,700t standard; 2,300t full load.
Dimensions: 312 oa x 39 x 14ft (95 x 12 x 4m).
Propulsion: 3-shaft CODAG 30,000bhp = 32kt.
Armament: *ASW:* two RBU 6000 mortars.
AAW: twin SA-N-4 launcher (18 missiles); four 76mm (2x2); four 30mm (2x2).
Sensors: *Surveillance:* Strut Curve.
Fire Control: one Pop Group, one Owl Screech, one Drum Tilt.
Sonars: HF hull-mounted.

The first Koni, built in the Black Sea in 1975-77, was thought to be the first of a class intended to replace the ageing Riga. Of the seven ships so far completed, however, no less than five have been transferred to allied or

Right: A Koni-class Patrol Ship in service with the East German Navy. Two units have been transferred to East Germany, one to Yugoslavia, one to Cuba, and two are reported to be building for Libya. The Koni has a heavy gun armament for its size, but antisubmarine capabilities are strictly limited, even by comparison with smaller Soviet coastal units.

Below: A Patrol Ship of the Koni class with a Soviet Navy pennant number. Only a single unit appears to be in service with the Soviet Navy, the remaining ships having been built for export.

friendly countries, and others are on order.

In appearance the Koni is not unlike the Grisha. It is, however, a much larger vessel, with higher freeboard and a built-up superstructure (which, taken together, suggest that the design may suffer from topweight problems).

Twin 76mm mountings are fitted fore and aft, with RBU 6000 mortars forward of the bridge and an SA-N-4 missile installation aft. Twin 30mm AA guns are fitted on either side of the bridge structure with a Drum Tilt radar between them.

The CODAG propulsion plant is thought to comprise two diesels for cruising, with a single large gas-turbine–probably the same model as that installed in the Kara and Krivak classes–for boost.

The Koni fits easily into the traditional Soviet SKR category. It has an adequate dual-purpose gun armament and is well provided with anti-air weapon systems for a ship of its size. ASW armament, however, is limited to the two somewhat dated mortars, allied to a small HF sonar. The adoption of a solid general-purpose armament rather than a weapons outfit tailored to a more specialized role adds weight to the theory that this class will not be built in large numbers for the Soviet Navy, and that it is primarily an export design.

Mirka I/II

Completed: 1964-67, Kaliningrad, Black Sea.
No. in class: Mirka I : 9. Mirka II : 9.
Displacement: 950t standard; 1,100t full load.
Dimensions: 266 oa x 30 x 10ft (81 x 9 x 3m).
Propulsion: 2-shaft CODOG; 24,000bhp = 32kt.
Armament: *ASW:* Four RBU 6000 (I) *or* two RBU 6000 (II); five 15.7in (400mm) TT (1x5, I) *or* ten 15.7in (400mm) TT (2x5, II).
AAW: four 76mm (2x2).
Sensors: *Surveillance:* Slim Net (I) *or* Strut Curve (II).
Fire Control: Hawk Screech.
Sonars: HF hull-mounted.

The Mirka class was built in the mid-1960s as a variation on the Petya. There were minor modifications to weapons and sensors, but the major change was in the layout of the propulsion machinery. A CODOG arrangement on only two shafts was adopted, the positions of the gas-turbines and diesels being reversed. In the Mirkas, the gas-turbines are located in the stern with the air intakes above them on a raised quarterdeck. Openings in the stern, closed by flaps when the ship is travelling at cruise speed, serve as exhausts. A lattice mast amidships replaces the funnel of the Petya.

Earlier units (now designated Mirka I) had a similar armament to the Petya I, except that the hand-loaded antisubmarine mortars were replaced by the automatic RBU 6000. Later units, the Mirka II group, however, were

Below: A profile view of the Mirka I-class SKR. Note the single bank of torpedo tubes and the second pair of A/S mortars abreast the prominent air intakes aft.

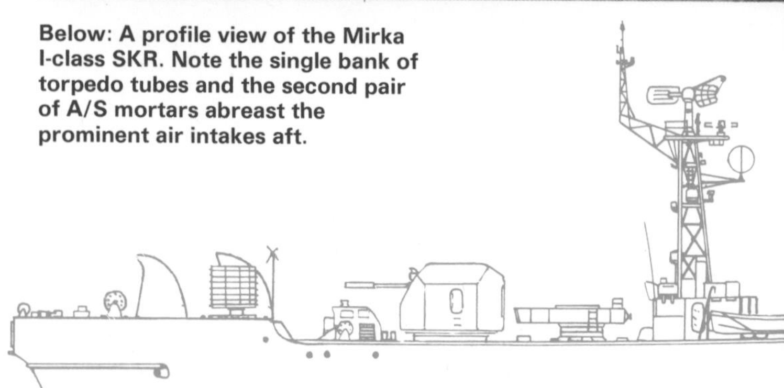

Above: A Patrol Ship of the Mirka II class in company with the cruiser *Moskva* and a support tanker in the Mediterranean.

modified in the same way as the contemporary Petya II: the after mortars were replaced by a second bank of torpedo tubes. A side-effect of the raised stern section was that it prevented the installation of the customary mine-rails. During the 1970s a number of ships were fitted with a dipping sonar on the port side of the transom, while others had it fitted abreast the bridge.

The Mirka class is deployed to all four Soviet fleets and shares the same missions as the Petya. Like the Petyas, the Mirkas were initially classified as Small ASW Ships (MPK) but are now rated Patrol Ships (SKR).

Above: A Patrol Ship of the Mirka II class underway. Note the two banks of torpedo tubes and the absence of A/S mortars aft, which distinguish the Mirka II.

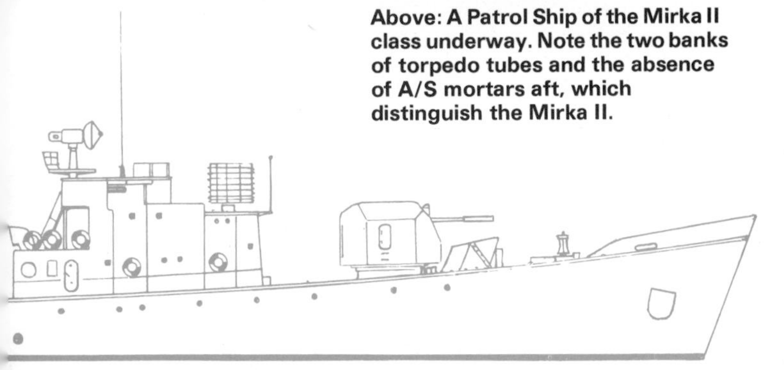

PATROL SHIP/SKR

Petya I/II

Completed: 1961-69, Kaliningrad; Black Sea; Komsomolsk.
No. in class: Petya I: 10, Petya I-Mod.: 10, Petya II: 26, Petya II-Mod.: 1.
Displacement: 950t standard; 1,100t full load.
Dimensions: 269 oa x 30 x 11ft (82 x 9 x 3m).
Propulsion: 3-shaft CODAG; 30,000bhp = 34kt.
Armament: *ASW:* four RBU 2500 (I); two RBU 2500 (I-Mod.); two RBU 6000 (II); five 15.7in (400mm) TT (1x5) (I); ten 15.7in (400mm) TT (2x5) (II).
AAW: four 76mm (2x2).
Sensors: *Surveillance:* Slim Net (I) *or* Strut Curve (II).
Fire Control: Hawk Screech.
Sonars: HF hull-mounted.

On completion, the first Petyas were designated Small ASW Ship (MPK). The class was designed primarily for operations in coastal waters: small size, lack of freeboard and low endurance make them unsuited to open-ocean operations. They have, nevertheless, frequently been deployed out of area, particularly in the Mediterranean.

The ASW armament of the first group of ships, Petya I, comprises four hand-loaded antisubmarine mortars, disposed at the forward end of the bridge structure and on the stern, and a quintuple bank of 15.7in (400mm) tubes for homing torpedoes. In the Petya II this was modified to include a second bank of tubes in place of the after group of mortars; the forward mortars were updated to the automatic RBU 6000 model. During the 1970s a number of Petya Is had their after mortars replaced by a housing for a variable depth sonar to complement the original hull-mounted sonar. These ships became known as the Petya I-Mod. A single Petya II has been similarly modified.

For anti-air defence twin 76mm mountings are fitted fore and aft, with a single FC director above the bridge.

The propulsion system is a combined gas-turbine and diesel installation. The configuration of the funnel suggests that two small-to-medium gas-turbines are used for boost. The single diesel, for which there are exhaust vents close to the waterline amidships, is used for cruising.

The Petya design is a simple one, well-suited to mass production. Petyas serve in all four Soviet fleets, where they have a variety of duties, including the escort of convoys or amphibious units and ASW and anti-surface patrol. In recognition of the importance of the anti-surface role, they have recently been redesignated SKR.

Above: A Petya II taking part in the world-wide Soviet Navy exercise OKEAN 70.

Above: Stern view of a Petya I with older-type RBU 2500 mortars forward of the bridge and on the stern. The low funnel is divided into twin uptakes for the gas turbine exhausts. The gas turbines are used only for boost.

Left: A Petya II, with two banks of torpedo tubes and two RBU 6000 mortars. Note the diesel exhaust from the hull vents.

PATROL SHIP/SKR

Riga

Completed: 1955-59, Kaliningrad; Nikolayev.
No. in class: 36.
Displacement: 1,000t standard; 1,420t full load.
Dimensions: 299 oa x 33 x 10ft (91 x 10 x 3m).
Propulsion: 2-shaft geared steam turbines; 20,000 shp = 28kt.
Armament: Three 100mm (3x1), four 37mm (2x2); four 25mm (2x2) (some ships only); two/three 21in (533mm) TT (1x2/3); two RBU 2500 *or* two RBU 1200.
Sensors: *Surveillance:* Slim Net.
Fire Control: Sun Visor.

As completed, the Riga was a traditional Soviet Patrol Ship, with a heavy conventional gun armament and a single bank of torpedo tubes. Compared with the two-funnelled Kola class which immediately preceded it, the Riga was an altogether more compact design, with hull-form and weight distribution well-adapted to good sea-keeping, and a reduction in the main armament from four guns to three.

Although quickly outdated, the Rigas have proved to be useful, seaworthy ships, and they have seen extensive service both in Soviet waters and out of area. Most were fitted with antisubmarine mortars shortly after completion, and some later had twin 25mm AA mountings added abreast the funnel. Two units have been fitted with a short lattice mast on the after superstructure for ECM antennae; they can also be distinguished by their raised funnel cowling.

Some 65 units of the Riga class were built, but a number were transferred to friends or allies during the 1960s and few remain in active service with the Soviet Navy.

Above: A Riga participating in OKEAN 70 photographed in the Philippine Sea by a US Navy photographer.

Below: A Riga underway. Few ships of the class have received any modernisation, and they may be considered outdated.

SMALL ROCKET SHIP/MRK

Nanuchka

Completed: 1979 onward, Petrovsky Yard (Leningrad).
No. in class: Nanuchka I: 16, Nanuchka III: 3 (+? building)
Displacement: 780t standard 930t full load.
Dimensions: 195 oa x 40 x 10ft (60 x 12 x 3m).
Propulsion: 3-shaft diesels; 30,000bhp = 32kt.
Armament: *SSM:* six SS-N-9 missiles (2x3)
AAW: twin SA-N-4 (18 missiles); two 57mm (1x2)

Below: Profile of a Nanuchka I. Note the prominent radome housing the Band Stand radar.

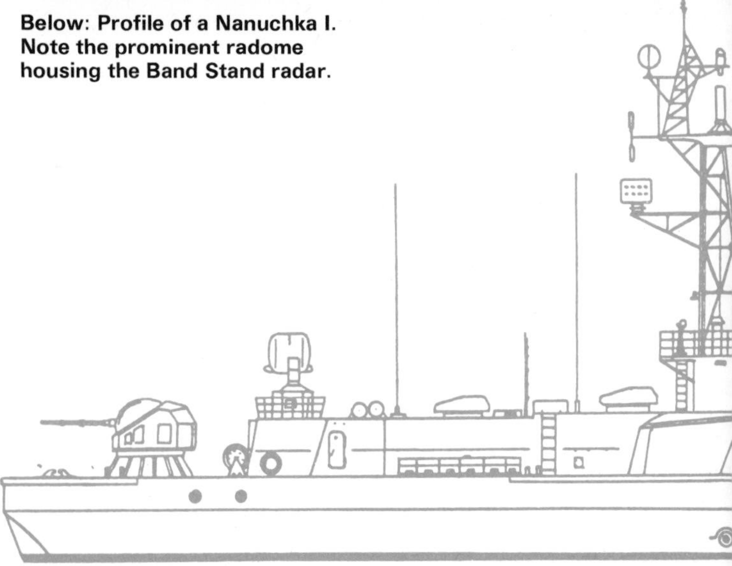

	(Nanuchka I); one 76mm; one 30mm gatling (Nanuchka III)
Sensors:	*Fire Control:* Band Stand, Pop Group, Muff Cob (I) *or* Bass Tilt (III).

The Nanuchka was intended to perform the same area-defence mission as the early missile destroyers of the Kildin and Krupny classes (which, in the late 1960s, were being converted to other roles as a result of the obsolescence of their SS-N-1 missile armament). Unlike its predecessors, the Nanuchka was an enlarged patrol boat design, with a low length-to-beam ratio. ▶

Above: A Nanuchka I photographed in 1977 with its twin 57mm mounting elevated.

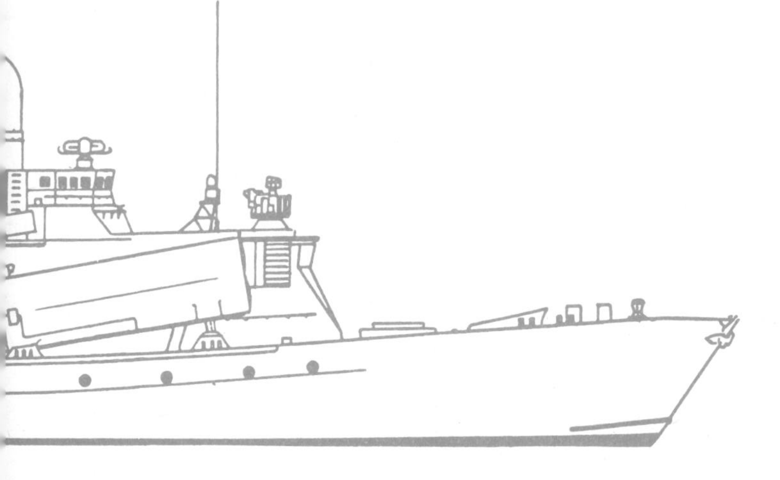

Above: A Nanuchka III—FC radar is Bass Tilt rather than Muff Cob, and a single 76mm gun replaces the twin 57mm mounting.

▶ The main armament comprises two triple launchers for SS-N-9 missiles, which are fitted on either side of a two-deck bridge structure. Guidance is by a Band Stand radar housed in a prominent radome just forward of the lattice mast. At longer ranges, targeting and mid-course guidance would be provided by aircraft.

AAW capabilities are on a par with the contemporary Grisha-class MPK: there is an SA-N-4 missile launcher forward of the bridge and a twin 57mm automatic mounting aft. In the Nanuchka III, which first appeared in 1978, the twin 57mm mounting is replaced by a single 76mm for improved performance against enemy FPBs. The Nanuchka III also has a 30mm gatling at the after end of the superstructure, and the original Muff Cob FC

Above: A Nanuchka I underway in the Baltic. The SS-N-9 triple launcher can be clearly seen beside the bridge.

director has been replaced by a Bass Tilt.

Although primarily designed to defend Soviet sea-space, the Nanuchkas have frequently been deployed out of area, especially in the Mediterranean, where they have combined with larger units to form anti-carrier task groups. They have been observed to roll badly in a seaway, and their propulsion machinery–comprising three sets of paired diesels–is unreliable. The continuing construction of the class at a rate of two boats per year is, however, testimony to the success of the large missile-boat concept.

Below: Overhead view of a Nanuchka I. The SA-N-4 "bin" can be seen forward of the bridge.

SMALL ROCKET SHIP/MRK

Tarantul

Completed: 1979 onward, Petrovsky Yard (Leningrad).
No. in class: 1 (+? building).
Displacement: 750t full load.
Dimensions: 184 oa x 34 x 8ft (56 x 11 x 2.5m).
Propulsion: 3-shaft COGAG; 36,000bhp = 35kt.
Armament: *SSM:* four SS-N-2C missiles (2x2).
AAW: one 76mm; two 30mm gatlings.
Sensors: *Surveillance:* Strut Curve (?).
Fire Control: Bass Tilt.

At first thought to be a successor to the Nanuchka, the Tarantul now appears to be a response to a different set of Staff Requirements, the nature of which is as yet unclear.

A major difference between the Tarantul and the Nanuchka classes is the propulsion system: in the Tarantul, the paired diesels of the Nanuchka have been replaced by gas-turbines on three shafts. This has effectively improved reaction time, while reducing range and endurance.

The other major difference lies in the anti-ship missile armament, which in the Tarantul comprises four SS-N-2C missiles, the paired launchers being fitted one above the other abreast the superstructure. Adoption of the horizon-range SS-N-2 missile in place of the 60nm (110km) SS-N-9 suggests that the Tarantul is not designed for the same area-defence mission as the Nanuchka.

MISSILE-BOAT/RKA

Matka

Completed: 1978 onward, Izhora Yard (Leningrad).
No. in class: 10 (+3 building).
Displacement: 215t standard; 250t full load.
Dimensions: 128 oa x 25 x 6ft (39 x 8 x 2m).
Propulsion: 3-shaft diesels; 15,000bhp = 40kt.
Armament: *SSM:* two SS-N-2C launchers.
AAW: one 76mm, one 30mm gatling.
Sensors: *Fire Control:* Bass Tilt.

The Matka is the missile counterpart of the Turya class torpedo-boat. It has the same basic Osa hull-form and propulsion system as the Turya and an identical hydrofoil system.

The major development as regards armament is the fitting of a single 76mm mounting of a new design forward. Prior to its adoption in the Matka and the Nanuchka III, the mounting underwent trials aboard the experimental patrol boat *Slepen* from 1975. It appears to have been developed as a counter to the OTO-Melara mounting of the same calibre adopted by the Federal German and Danish navies for their missile-boats and corvettes.

In order to compensate for the additional weight of the 76mm mounting, the number of anti-ship missile launchers has been reduced from four to two–although the missile is the "C" version of the SS-N-2, with improved homing. The launchers are fitted well aft to give added "lift" to the bow. Between them is a single 30mm gatling. A Bass Tilt radar at the after end of the bridge controls both the 76mm and 30mm mountings. The suppression of two of the missile launchers has allowed the bridge structure to be extended out towards the sides of the ship, providing improved operational spaces in comparison with previous classes.

The Matka has now entered series production and is being built at the rate of three boats per year. Matkas will supplement the Osa class boats.

Above: An MRK of the Tarantul class. It is not yet clear whether this design will enter series production.

The remaining weapons are similar to those of the Nanuchka III, although, significantly, the SA-N-4 launcher has been discarded. The single 76mm mounting on the fore-deck enjoys exceptionally good arcs because of the adoption of a more compact superstructure. Twin 30mm gatlings are mounted side by side at the after end of the superstructure.

It is possible that the Tarantul may be employed as leader of the missile/torpedo-boat flotillas. High speed, together with larger operational spaces and an armament similar to that of the Matka-class missile boats would make the Tarantul well-suited to this role. Alternatively, it may be an experimental design intended primarily for export.

Above: A missile boat of the Matka class alongside.

Below: A Matka at speed. The SS-N-2C launchers are close to the stern. The surveillance radar does not appear to have been installed in this vessel.

Sarancha

Completed: 1977 onward, Petrovsky Yard (Leningrad).
No. in class: 3 (+ ? building).
Displacement: 300t full load.
Dimensions: 148 oa x 36 x 9ft (45 x 11 x 2.8m).
Propulsion: 2-shaft COGAG; 24,000bhp = 45kt.
Armament: *SSM:* four SS-N-9 missiles (2x2).
AAW: twin SA-N-4 launcher (18 missiles); one 30mm gatling.
Sensors: *Surveillance:* Fish Bowl.
Fire Control: Band Stand, Bass Tilt.

The Sarancha may have been envisaged as a hydrofoil successor to the Nanuchka. The adoption of a combination of foils and gas-turbines suggests an emphasis on quick reaction times rather than endurance. Instead of patrolling the periphery of Soviet sea-space to prevent incursions by hostile surface units, the Sarancha would presumably be deployed to strategically-placed harbours to make high-speed sorties to intercept contacts made by aerial reconnaissance.

Evidence that such a mission is envisaged for the Sarancha rests in its medium-range missile armament. Two pairs of elevating launchers for SS-N-9 missiles are fitted on either side of the bridge; and these would require relay aircraft for guidance beyond horizon range. The Sarancha is also fitted, like the Nanuchkas, with an SA-N-4 air defence system, and it has a 30mm gatling at the after end of the superstructure.

It is not yet clear whether the Sarancha will enter series production or

Below: A Sarancha foilborne. The twin exhausts for the gas-turbines are especially clear in this view.

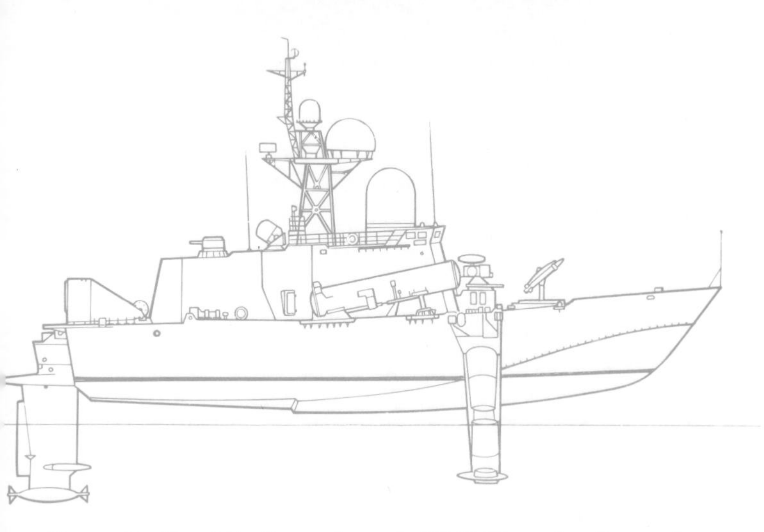

Above: Profile of the Sarancha; note SA-N-4 launcher forward.

whether it is simply a prototype. It has only one-quarter the displacement of the Nanuchka and may have proved itself too small for the area defence role. The Saranchas would also be incapable of the long-range deployments frequently undertaken by the Nanuchkas: construction of the latter class, has, therefore, continued at the same Petrovsky Yard as the Sarancha throughout the late 1970's.

MISSILE-BOAT/RK

Osa I/II

Completed: 1959-70, various yards.
No. in class: Osa I : 70. Osa II : 45.
Displacement: Osa I: 175t standard; 210t full load.
Osa II: 215t standard; 245t full load.
Dimensions: 128 oa x 25 x 6ft (39 x 8 x 2m).
Propulsion: 3-shaft diesels; 12,000bhp (I) *or* 15,000bhp (II) = 36kt.
Armament: *SSM:* four SS-N-2A/B missiles (4x1).
AAW: four 30mm (2x2); SA-N-5 launcher (some boats only).
Sensors: *Surveillance:* Square Tie.
Fire Control: Drum Tilt.

The Osa was the Soviet Navy's first purpose-built missile boat, the earlier Komar class having been a stop-gap conversion of the P-6 torpedo-boats. In comparison with the Komar, displacement was doubled and a steel hull was adopted to provide the necessary strength, resulting in a far more seaworthy craft. The adoption of the basic Osa hull-form in subsequent classes, such as the Shershen, Stenka, Turya and Matka, is clear testimony to its success.

The profile of the Osa I is dominated by the four massive box launchers for the SS-N-2 anti-ship missile, disposed two on either side of a long, enclosed, single deck-high superstructure. The launchers, in fixed positions, are arranged in such a way that the second pair, elevated at an angle of 15°, fire over the forward pair, angled at 12°. Unlike the missile launchers on the ▶

Below: An Osa I at speed. The missile boats generally operate with torpedo boats in mixed squadrons. A crew member gives scale to the large SS-N-2 box launchers.

Above: A Styx missile is launched from an Osa I.

Left: An Osa II at Leningrad. The ribbed launchers contain the B version of the SS-N-2 Styx missile, which has improved homing.

▶Komar, those on the Osa are completely enclosed, with a hinged flap at the forward end for firing or reloading. Aft of the launchers are curved blast shields to deflect the missile exhaust outward. Twin 30mm mountings are fitted fore and aft, with a Drum Tilt director on a pedestal above the after mounting. The remaining electronics are carried on a single pole mast just aft of the bridge. Some Osa I boats have missile launchers which are slightly longer than the standard model: on these, the after 30mm has been raised on its pedestal.

Right: An Osa I at speed. These craft are capable of a maximum speed of some 36kt.

Below: An Osa II under tow by a Soviet tug in the Atlantic en route to Cuba. The cylindrical ribbed launchers distinguish the second Osa group from the first.

Below: Two vessels of the Osa I class alongside.

In the late 1960s a number of units were converted to Osa II configuration. The main modification was the fitting of the SS-N-2B missile, with an improved homing head. The Osa II can be easily distinguished from the Osa I by its small, cylindrical, ribbed launchers.

The Osa, although now succeeded in production by the Matka, still constitutes the backbone of the Soviet coastal missile forces and has been widely exported to friends and allies. The Soviet units operate with the torpedo-boats in combined flotillas and, in the event of hostilities, would perform a variety of tasks. These would include the defence of Warsaw Pact territory and the seaward flanks of the armies; the protection of amphibious and mine-laying operations against enemy missile craft; and the disruption of enemy coastal shipping. If opposed by NATO fast attack craft, the Soviet boats would rely on numbers rather than sophistication for the success of their missions.

TORPEDO-BOAT/TKA

Turya

Completed:	1974 onward, various yards.
No. in class:	30.
Displacement:	205t standard; 240t full load.
Dimensions:	128 oa x 25 x 6ft (39 x 8 x 2m).
Propulsion:	3-shaft diesels; 15,000bhp = 40kt.
Armament:	Four 21in (533mm) TT (4x1).
	AAW: two 57mm (1x2); two 25mm (1x2).
Sensors:	*Surveillance:* Pot Drum.
	Fire Control: Muff Cob.

The Turya followed on from the Shershen as the standard Soviet torpedo-boat. While retaining the basic Osa hull-form common to virtually all Soviet small construction throughout the 1960s and 1970s, the Turya has a pair of semi-submerged hydrofoils forward, to lift and stabilise the bow as the boat

Below: Profile of the Turya-class torpedo hydrofoil. The basic Osa hull form is retained, but semi-submerged hydrofoils are fitted.

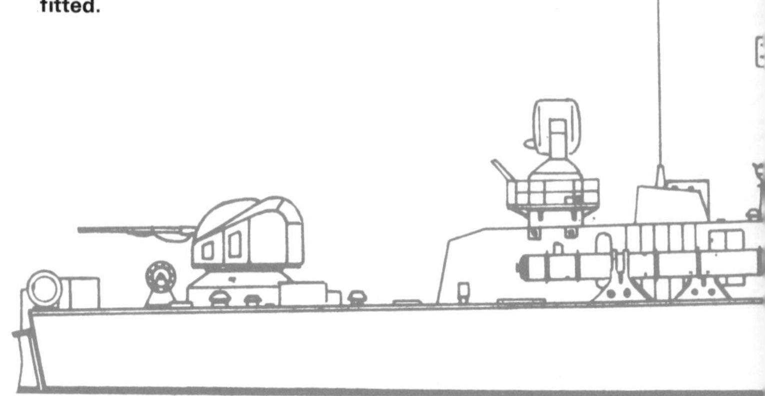

planes on the water. This is not a true hydrofoil arrangement; the foils form an arc or trapezoid shape and are braced against the hull at their mid-point.

The general balance and layout of the armament of the Shershen is retained in the Turya, although the mine-rails and depth charge racks aft have been discarded in favour of a Hormone dipping sonar to starboard—a curious development in view of the total absence of ASW weapons. The major modification, however, is the installation of a twin 57mm automatic mounting aft, with the Drum Tilt FC director of the Shershen being replaced by a Muff Cob. The feasibility of installing such a large gun mounting on a small craft was tested aboard the experimental FPB *Slepen* (a modified Osa), which had the 57mm mounting installed forward of the bridge when completed in 1970. The repositioning of this mounting aft in the Turya was necessitated by the adoption of hydrofoils. The effect of the installation, which is counter-balanced forward only by a small, obsolescent, twin 25mm mounting, is to shift the balance aft.

The Turya is being built in similar numbers to the Shershen and performs an identical mission. Its missile counterpart is the Matka.

Above: A Turya underway. Note the large twin 57mm automatic mounting on the stern. The Muff Cob FC director is at the after end of the superstructure.

TORPEDO-BOAT/TKA

Shershen

Completed: 1962-74, various yards.
No. in class: 30.
Displacement: 150t standard; 180t full load.
Dimensions: 112 oa x 23 x 5ft (34 x 7 x 1.5m).
Propulsion: 3-shaft diesels; 12,000bhp = 38kt.
Armament: Four 21in (533mm) TT (4x1).
AAW: four 30mm (2x2).
Sensors: *Surveillance:* Pot Drum.
Fire Control: Drum Tilt.

The Shershen was the first large torpedo-boat built for the Soviet Navy. The design was based on that of the Osa class missile boat, with which the Shershen shares a similar hull-form and an identical all-diesel propulsion system.

The four side-mounted missile launchers of the Osa were replaced by single 21in (533mm) torpedo tubes, angled out at about 8° to the boat's axis. Like the Osa, the Shershen has twin 30mm mountings fore and aft controlled by a prominent Drum Tilt director. The increase in available deck-space made it possible to fit depth charge racks and mine-rails. These boats are, therefore, equally capable of high-speed minelaying raids and of employment as high-speed subchasers.

The Shershen is designed to operate alongside the Osa in combined missile/torpedo-boat flotillas. The Osa class boats would fire off their missiles at an enemy force and the Shershen class boats would then move in, taking advantage of confusion in the enemy formation caused by the missile attacks.

In addition to the boats built for the Soviet Navy, large numbers have been transferred to other allied or friendly countries. Most serve in the Baltic and the Black Sea, where their opponents in the event of hostilities would be similar-sized NATO craft.

Above: A 533mm torpedo being loaded aboard a Shershen in service with the East German Navy.

Left: A Shershen launches two of its four 533mm torpedoes.

Mine Warfare (MCM) Craft

In spite of the importance to the Soviet Navy of defensive and offensive minelaying, the only specialized minelayers built for the Soviet Navy are three units of the Alesha (or Alyosha) class. Since the Aleshas also appear to serve as minesweeper support ships there is some doubt as to their exact designation, which may be Minelayer (*Zagraditel'*

MINELAYER/ZM

Alesha

Completed: 1965-69, Black Sea.
Names: *Pripyat* (+ 2).
Displacement: 2,900t standard; 3,500t full load.
Dimensions: 345 oa x 48 x 16ft (98 x 15 x 5m).
Propulsion: 2-shaft diesels; 8,000bhp = 20kt.
Armament: Four 57mm (1x4).
Sensors: *Surveillance:* Strut Curve.
Fire Control: Muff Cob.

Right: A minelayer of the Alesha class at sea. This unit has a crane forward of the bridge, whereas the other two ships have twin derricks. Note the quadruple 57mm mounting on the forecastle and the Muff Cob FC director above the bridge. Running aft from the single superstructure block is a complex of rails, which besides accommodating mines is also presumably used for the transfer of stores which can be wheeled around the deck on trolleys before being tansferred by derrick to smaller vessels lying alongside. It is thought that in peacetime the Aleshas serve as netlayers.

Minny, ZM) or Depot Ship (PB).

Many Soviet minesweepers have a subsidiary minelaying role; this may account, in part, for the continued construction of large ocean-going sweepers throughout the 1960s and 1970s. Three categories of minesweeper have therefore been maintained, and these correspond roughly to the Ocean/Coastal/Inshore categories which formed the basis of the NATO MCM programme of the 1950s. The three Soviet categories are:

Morskoy Tral'shchik (MT), Seagoing Minesweeper; _Bazovy Tral'shchik_ (BT), Base Minesweeper; _Reydovoy Tral'shchik_ (RT), Roadstead Minesweeper.

The Alesha is a multi-purpose vessel, apparently with a primary minelaying role and subsidiary roles as a netlayer and as a minesweeper support ship.

The after part is taken up by rails for an estimated 400 mines and winches and cranes for handling nets and booms. The stern, which is built around a ramp with a large gantry above it, resembles that of a whale factory ship.

At either end of the compact superstructure there are paired derricks—at least one Alesha has a single crane in place of the forward pair—for handling cargo and supplies.

For self-defence the Alesha carries a quadruple 57mm mounting on a deckhouse forward, controlled by a Muff Cob director above the bridge. In peacetime the Aleshas appear to serve in the role of boom defence vessels, defending Soviet harbours against incursions by submarines.

Natya

Completed: 1970 onward, various yards.
No. in class: 30.
Displacement: 650t standard; 750t full load.
Dimensions: 200 oa x 32 x 8ft (61 x 10 x 2.5m).
Propulsion: 2-shaft diesels; 4,000bhp = 18kt.
Armament: *ASW:* two RBU 1200 mortars.
AAW: four 30mm (2x2); four 25mm (2x2).
Sensors: *Fire Control:* Drum Tilt.

The Natya is the successor to the Yurka class. The design adheres to the traditional Soviet concept of the large steel-hulled ocean minesweeper capable of performing a variety of roles, including that of coastal ASW. Length and displacement have been significantly increased from those of the Yurka to accommodate a more comprehensive armament: as well as the twin 30mm, there are twin 25mm mountings in echelon on either side of the funnel, and RBU 1200 antisubmarine mortars are fitted forward of the bridge.

An interesting feature of the sweep-handling arrangements is the trawler-style ramp cut into the stern, bridged by a narrow catwalk. This facilitates bringing aboard the exceptionally bulky sweep gear. Early Natyas have rigid davits, but in later units these are articulated.

Minesweepers of the Natya class have been deployed to the Mediterranean, the Indian Ocean and the South Atlantic.

Above: A Natya-class ocean minesweeper at sea. The sweep-handling arrangements are mounted at the stern.

Below: A Natya photographed in the English Channel. A shrouded RBU 1200 mortar can be seen forward of the bridge.

OCEAN MINESWEEPER/MT

Yurka

Completed: 1964-70, various yards.
No. in class: 48.
Displacement: 400t standard; 460t full load.
Dimensions: 171 oa x 31 x 7ft (52 x 9 x 2m).
Propulsion: 2-shaft diesels; 4,000bhp = 18kt.
Armament: Four 30mm (2x2).
Sensors: *Fire Control:* Drum Tilt.

The Yurka followed on from the T 43 class as the standard Soviet ocean minesweeper. Although length and displacement were almost identical to those of the T 43, a hull-form with a much fuller waterplane was adopted, improving stability and at the same time compensating for the increase in freeboard amidships. The hull is thought to be of aluminium alloy. The canted funnel is of similar configuration to those of the Kynda class RKRs, with twin exhausts for the diesels side by side.

The winches for the sweep gear are exceptionally large and twin floats are stowed just aft of the break in the forecastle. Twin 30mm guns are fitted fore and aft and the Drum Tilt FC director is carried high on a slender lattice foremast.

Above: A Yurka-class minesweeper at anchor. The high freeboard is especially noteworthy.

Below: Profile view of a Yurka-class MT.

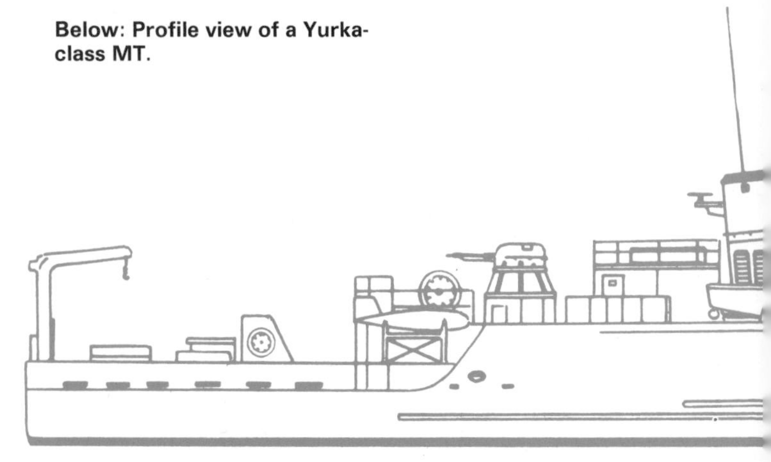

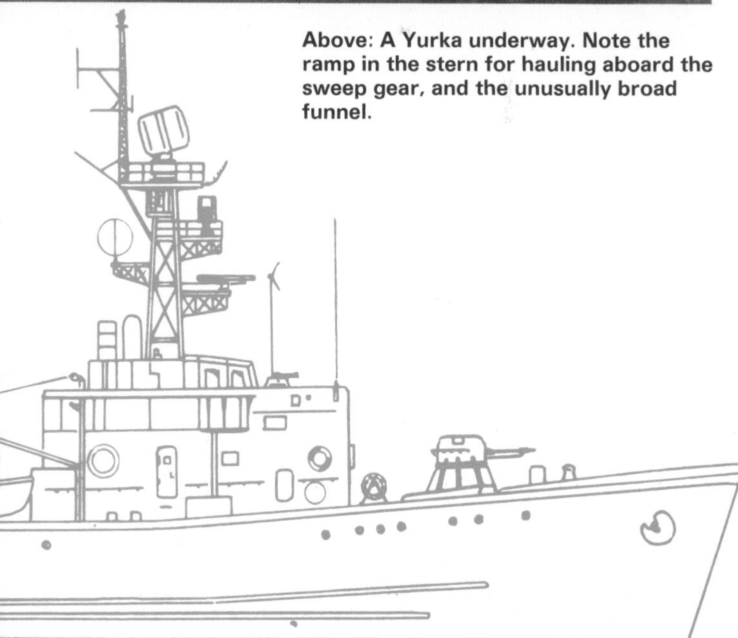

Above: A Yurka underway. Note the ramp in the stern for hauling aboard the sweep gear, and the unusually broad funnel.

Sonya and Zhenya

Completed: Sonya: 1974 onward, various yards.
Zhenya: 1973.
No. in class: Sonya: 35.
Zhenya: 4.
Displacement: Sonya: 350t standard; 400t full load.
Zhenya: 220t standard; 300t full load.
Dimensions: Sonya: 159 oa x 25 x 6ft (49 x 8 x 2m).
Zhenya: 141 oa x 25 x 6ft (43 x 8 x 2m).
Propulsion: Sonya/Zhenya: 2-shaft diesels; 2,400bhp = 18kt.
Armament: Sonya: two 30mm (1x2); two 25mm (1x2).
Zhenya: two 30mm (1x2).

The Sonya and Zhenya classes are successors to the Vanya class. They have a hull-form clearly derived from the Vanya and a similar block superstructure surmounted by a tall lattice mast. There are, however, significant differences, including the reversion in the Sonya and Zhenya to a conventional funnel for the diesel exhausts, and the provision of an optical fire control position forward of the bridge.

The Zhenya has a hull of glass-reinforced plastic (GRP). This method of construction does not appear to have been successful, for only four units of the class were built.

The units of the Sonya class, which followed, have a wooden hull with a GRP coating: the use of wood as the main hull material gives improved stability, while the GRP coating reduces maintenance. Other modifications are the addition of a twin 25mm abaft the funnel and a single large articulated davit for the sweep gear, in place of the twin rigid davits of the Zhenya. The Sonya, evidently a more successful design than the experimental Zhenya, has entered series production.

Above: A Sonya-class BT underway. The Sonya is currently the standard Soviet coastal minesweeper.

Although the Sonya is described as a "minehunter" in some reference books, there is nothing to suggest that the class is fitted with the minehunting sonars and remote-control mine disposal vehicles of its Western counterparts. An alternative, and more likely, method to be employed by the Sonya in this role is the use of streamed TV apparatus to monitor the seabed and divers to place charges.

Below: A Zhenya-class BT photographed in 1975. The Zhenya is thought to be the only major type of Soviet minesweeper with an all-glass-reinforced plastic hull.

Vanya

Completed: 1961-73, various yards.
No. in class: 70.
Displacement: 200t standard; 245t full load.
Dimensions: 131 oa x 24 x 6ft (40 x 7 x 2m).
Propulsion: 2-shaft diesels; 2,200bhp = 18kt.
Armament: Two 30mm (1x2).

The Vanya, which succeeded the steel-hulled Sasha class, was a completely new design and was clearly influenced by the coastal minesweepers built by NATO countries during the late 1950s. It was the first Soviet minesweeper to employ wooden hull construction. The forecastle, combining high freeboard with an almost total absence of sheer, is carried well aft, and the sweep-handling gear is accommodated on a short quarterdeck aft of the break. There is no funnel: the diesel exhaust are released through vents in the hull.

Like its NATO counterparts, the Vanya was a specialist minesweeper from

the outset: a light twin 30mm forward comprises the only gun armament and there is no FC director.

In 1974 one boat was converted to a minehunter configuration. A mine-hunting sonar is thought to have been fitted, and the bridge has been extended forward, presumably to provide the additional space necessary for monitoring underwater operations. To compensate for the forward extension of the bridge, a twin 25mm moutning was fitted in place of the 30mm. The sweep gear was replaced by a whaler on davits and a new lattice mainmast carrying a variety of electronic antennae was fitted. Mine disposal by divers is the most likely minehunting technique; the additional electronics may be for radio guidance of the small Ilyusha class minesweepers, also completed in the early 1970s, which are thought to be capable of unmanned operation in remote control. Two more Vanyas may have been similarly modified, but the slow conversion rate suggests that the modification is part of an experimental programme.

Below: The Vanya was the standard Soviet coastal minesweeper of the 1960s. Large numbers were built during the 1960s and early 1970s, the class now numbering 70 vessels.

COASTAL MINESWEEPER/RT

Sasha

Completed: 1956-60, unknown yard(s).
No. in class: 8.
Displacement: 250t standard; 280t full load.
Dimensions: 150 oa x 21 x 7ft (45 x 6 x 2m).
Propulsion: 2-shaft diesels; 2,200bhp = 18kt.
Armament: One 57mm; four 25mm (2x2).

Below: An RT of the Sasha class underway.

SPECIAL SERVICE MINESWEEPER/(?)

Andryusha

Completed: 1975, unknown yard(s).
No. in class: 3.
Displacement: 320t standard; 360t full load.
Dimensions: 147 oa x 27 x 7ft (45 x 8 x 2m).
Propulsion: 2-shaft diesels; 2,200bhp = 15kt.
Armament: None.

The Andryusha class is outside the mainstream of Soviet MCM construction. Only three units have been built and they carry none of the usual sweep gear. Large twin cable ducts emerge from the forecastle just forward of the bridge and run all the way aft to the stern. The funnel is thought to contain uptakes for turbine generators, since the propulsion diesels vent their own exhausts through the sides of the hull. The hull itself is almost certainly of GRP to give the lowest possible magnetic signature. Taken together, these features suggest that the Andryusha is designed to counter magnetic mines, using its

The Sasha class minesweepers, built in the late 1950s and early 1960s, are unusual in having flush-decked hulls, the low freeboard aft being compensated by the considerable sheer forward. The sweep deck begins immediately aft of the funnel. They were the last Soviet coastal minesweepers to be constructed of steel. The heavy gun armament, enabling them to double as patrol boats, comprises a single 57mm forward and two twin 25mm at the after end of the bridge structure.

The Sasha class is now being withdrawn from service, and must certainly be regarded as obsolescent.

generators to pass a current through the cables and thus set up a powerful magnetic field.

Below: Profile of the Andryusha. The long cable ducts extend from the bridge to the stern on the vessel.

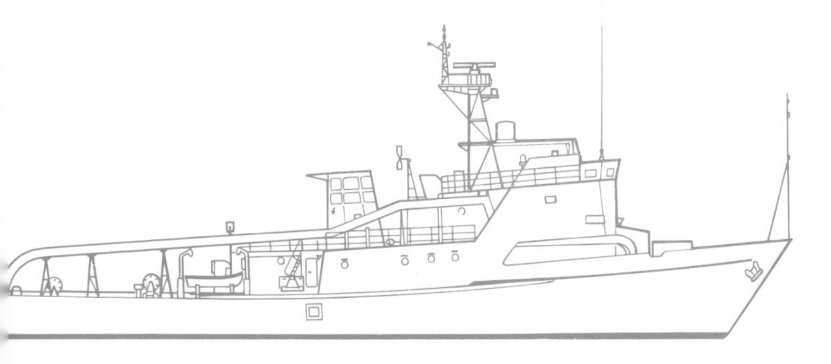

Amphibious Vessels

With the single exception of the recently-completed *Ivan Rogov,* the Soviet amphibious fleet is composed entirely of tank landing ships and smaller, independent landing craft (some of which are ACVs). The major vessels which appear in this section come under one of two categories:

> ***Bol'shoy Desantny Korabl'* (BDK), Large Landing Ship; *Sredny Desantny Korabl'* (SDK), Medium Landing Ship.**

Of the smaller landing craft, only the new LCMs of the Ondatra class can be accommodated in the larger landing ships, and then only by *Ivan Rogov* which can also operate ACVs from her docking well.

LARGE LANDING SHIP/BDK

Ivan Rogov

Completed: 1978 onward, Kaliningrad.
Names: *Ivan Rogov* (+ 1 building).
Displacement: 11,000t standard; 12,500t full load.
Dimensions: 522 oa x 80 x 21/28ft (159 x 25 x 6.5/8.5m).
Propulsion: 2-shaft COGAG; 24,000bhp = 20kt.
Armament: *Aircraft:* five Hormone A helicopters.
AA W: twin SA-N-4 launcher (18 missiles); two 76mm (1x2); four 30mm gatlings.
Shore Bombardment: one rocket launcher (1x20 barrels).
Sensors: *Surveillance:* Head Net C.
Fire Control: one Pop Group, one Owl Screech, two Bass Tilt.

▶

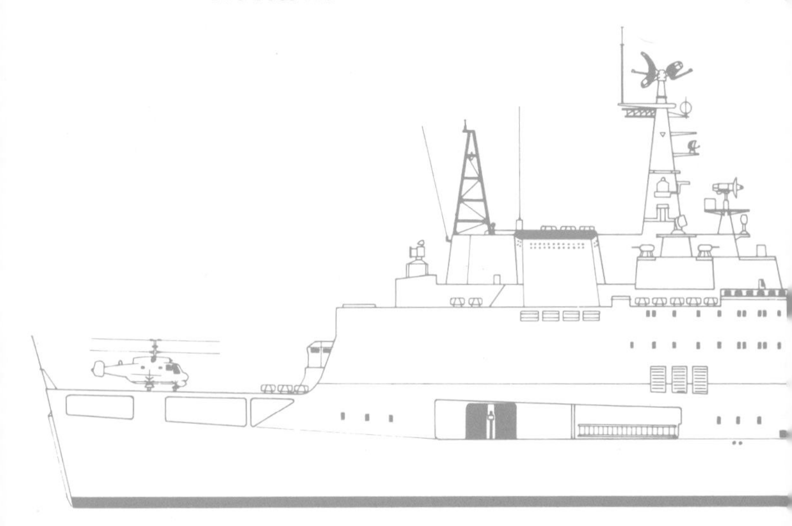

Above: A BTR-60PB amphibious personnel carrier comes ashore from a Soviet landing ship.

Right: A stern view of *Ivan Rogov.* A Ka-25 Hormone is on the after landing pad and the hangar doors are open. Note the large hinged stern ramp, which gives access to the docking well for ACVs or conventional landing craft.

Below: Profile of *Ivan Rogov.* The massive block superstructure (which includes four-decks-high troop accommodation) is particularly evident in this view.

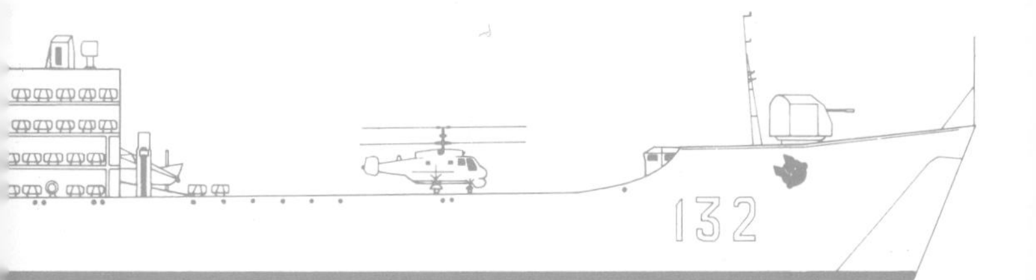

▶ Although *Ivan Rogov* carries the same BDK designation as the Alligator class, her displacement is more than twice that of her predecessor. More importantly, the design represents a significant break with previous Soviet amphibious ships in that it incorporates a hangar for helicopters and a docking-well for amphibious landing craft–both features of Western amphibious construction, but never before adopted by the Soviet Navy. The result is a ship capable not only of direct beach assault but also of both "horizontal" and "vertical" landing operations.

The lower part of the ship is built around a continuous tank deck, with workshops and accommodation to the sides and the traditional bow doors and ramp of an LST. Capacity is estimated at 10 tanks, plus 30 APCs and other vehicles. The vehicle load can be increased by utilising the midships section of the upper deck, access to which is gained by lowering a hinged ramp located immediately aft of the break in the forecastle.

At the after end of the ship the tank deck leads down into a docking-well some 98ft (30m) long and 66ft (20m) wide, closed by a large stern gate. An unusual feature of the docking-well is that the height of the deckhead rises towards the stern. This enables the *Rogov* to operate ACVs of the Gus or Lebed classes, both of which have tall tail rudders. Two ACVs can be accommodated side by side, with an alternative loading of the new Ondatra class LCMs, which are thought to have been designed specifically for *Rogov* and her successors.

The upper part of the ship is dominated by a massive block superstructure which extends to the sides of the ship. Apart from carrying the major defensive weapon systems and sensors, the superstructure has troop accommodation four decks high for a full battalion of Naval Infantry (522 officers and men) and also contains a large hangar for Ka-25 Hormone helicopters which appear to be fitted to serve in both the ASW and the troop-carrying roles. The hangar itself runs between the funnel uptakes, opening out into a wide bay offset to starboard at its after end. The sloping hangar floor is a continuation of the raised helicopter platform aft, and at its forward end leads down onto the main section of the upper deck via a fixed ramp. Helicopter take-off and landing spots, each with its own flying control cabin, are marked out aft of the break in the forecastle and above the stern.

AAW capabilities are exceptionally complete for an amphibious vessel, comprising an SA-N-4 missile launcher at the after end of the superstructure; a twin 76mm mounting on the forecastle, and 30mm gatlings on either side of the foremast. Forward of the main superstructure block to starboard is a tall, narrow deckhouse, on top of which is a rocket launcher for shore bombardment.

Above: The bulky superstructure of *Ivan Rogov* contains the helicopter hangar, as well as the accommodation for troops, who may number up to 522 officers and men.

The construction of *Ivan Rogov* marks a significant advance in the long-range amphibious capabilities of the Soviet Navy. However, the attempt to put the capabilities of the LPH, LPD and LST into one hull does not appear to be entirely successful. The docking-well is small by Western standards, and the ability to land heavy vehicles except by direct beaching is strictly limited; helicopter capacity is also somewhat limited (and the Ka-25 is not a specialist troop-carrying helicopter); and the increase in size has made beaching a more difficult and more hazardous operation. *Rogov* may be designed for single-ship operations in support of Soviet foreign policy; and although a second unit is reported as being under construction, series production is unlikely.

Below: The forward and after landing pads are clearly visible in this aerial view of *Ivan Rogov,* as is the rise of the deckhead towards the stern.

LARGE LANDING SHIP/BDK

Alligator

Completed: 1966-77, Kaliningrad.
Names: Type I: *Tomsky Komsomolets, Voronezhky Komsomolets, Krymsky Komsomolets* (+1).
Type II: *Sergei Lazo* (+1).
Type III: *Aleksandr Tortsev, Donetsky Shakhter, Krasnaya Presnya, Pyotr Ilichev, 50 Let Sheftsva VLKSM* (+1).
Type IV: *Nikolai Vilkov, Nikolai Filchenkov.*
Displacement: 3,400t standard; 4,500t full load.
Dimensions: 374 oa x 51 x 15ft (114 x 16 x 4.5m).
Propulsion: 2-shaft diesels; 8,000bhp = 18kt.
Armament: Two 57mm (1x2); two/four 25mm (1/2x2); rocket launcher (Type III ships).

The Alligator class, the first unit of which was completed shortly after the Polnocny went into production, was (unlike the Polish-built SDKs) built in the Soviet Union and constituted a break with the traditional Soviet LST in both conception and configuration. Not only is the Alligator clearly an ocean-going type, it also displays many features more often associated with mercantile construction. Early units had three large mercantile holds forward and a fourth smaller hold aft, each served by a crane. Together with the capacious stowage for vehicles and/or cargo on the upper deck, this suggests that the Alligator was designed from the outset as a long-range logistics vessel, built primarily for supply operations with only a secondary assault mission. This supposition has been borne out by the frequent use made of Alligator class ships to transport vehicles and equipment to friendly countries in Africa.

Below: An Alligator at anchor in the Mediterranean. The vessel alongside is an AGI.

Above: An Alligator II landing ship underway.

The tank deck itself is continuous, unlike that of previous Soviet LSTs, and has ramps at either end. It must, therefore, pass between twin uptakes combined in the exceptionally wide funnel. The Alligator is thought to have a load capacity of about 1,500 tons. Naval Infantry units are generally embarked on distant deployments, but troop capacity must be somewhat limited.

In later ships of the class, the forward and after hatches have been suppressed and the remaining two forward are served by a single crane. Some ships have a deckhouse forward on which a rocket launcher and/or twin 25mm AA guns have been installed. SA-N-5 missile launchers are now being fitted. These modifications have resulted in some improvement in assault capabilities, without seriously affecting performance in the logistics role.

Ropucha

Completed: 1975 onward, Gdansk (Poland).
No. in class: 11.
Displacement: 3,450t standard; 4,400t full load.
Dimensions: 360 oa x 49 x 12ft (110 x 15 x 3.5m).
Propulsion: 2-shaft diesels; 10,000bhp = 17kt.
Armament: Four 57mm (2x2).
Sensors: *Surveillance:* Strut Curve.
Fire Control: Muff Cob.

Built, like the Polnocny class, in Poland, the Ropucha is altogether larger and more capable than its predecessor. The main improvements, apart from the increase in vehicle capacity resulting from the increase in size, lie in the powerful modern anti-aircraft armament and the extensive troop accommodation.

The tank deck is continuous, with bow and stern ramps provided. Above the squared-off bow section is a long, sliding, hatch cover for alongside loading or off-loading of vehicles and supplies.

The conventional LST hull-form is surmounted by an exceptionally long superstructure with accommodation for large numbers of troops. At either end of the superstructure are twin 57mm automatic mountings, controlled by a single Muff Cob director. Air search and navigation radars are carried atop a tall lattice foremast. Forward of the bridge there appears to be provision for the installation of an SA-N-4 "bin" launcher—although the associated Pop Group guidance radar is not fitted.

The relatively slow building rate of the Ropucha class and the transfer of two units to friendly countries is puzzling: it may indicate that the Soviets are looking increasingly to large high-speed ACVs to perform short-range assault missions in areas such as the Baltic and Black Sea.

Below: The Ropucha is more heavily armed than previous Soviet landing ships. Twin 57mm mountings are fitted fore and aft.

Above: Stern view of a Ropucha. Note the stern gate, the split funnels and the hatch on the forecastle.

MEDIUM LANDING SHIP/SDK

Polnocny

Completed: 1964 onward, Gdansk (Poland).
No. in class: 52.
Displacement: 700-1,000t standard; 920-1,250t full load.
Dimensions: 240-269 oa x 29-33 x 6ft (73-82 x 9-10 x 2m).
Propulsion: 2-shaft diesels; 5,000bhp = 18kt.
Armament: Two/four 30mm (1/2x2); two rocket launchers.
Sensors: *Fire Control:* Drum Tilt.

The Polnocny class, which entered series production in the early 1960s, is the standard Soviet landing ship. Its small size and low freeboard serve to emphasise the fact that the Soviet amphibious forces are designed for short-range operations.

The Polnocny is a conventional LST built around a long tank deck, with the superstructure and propulsion machinery well aft. Tanks and APCs are landed via bow doors and a ramp. There is a long, sliding hatch over the bow section for loading stores and vehicles.

Improvements have been made throughout the series and there are a number of different sub-groups within the class. Modifications to the hull include a more angular stem, for better sea-keeping, and degaussing cables. The Polnocny III has a 20ft (6m) section inserted forward of the bridge and

Above: Close-up of the helicopter platform fitted on at least one of the more recent Polnocny-class landing ships. There is no hangar.

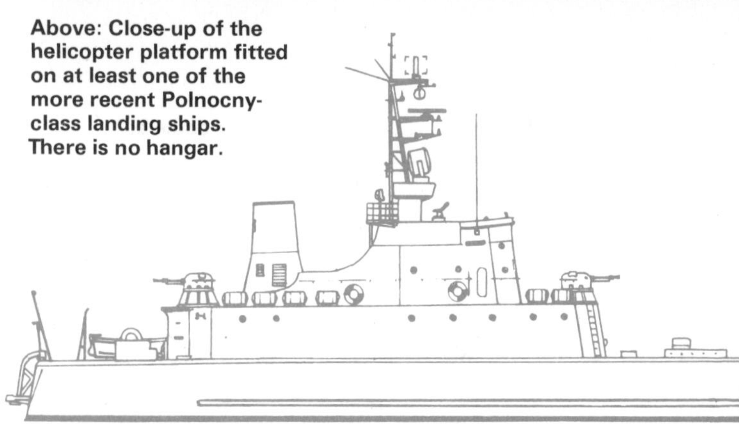

Above: A Polnocny III fitted with a helicopter platform forward of the bridge. Note the rocket launchers for fire support.

can accommodate eight APCs, compared with six in earlier units.

There are also considerable variations within the class in the length and shape of the superstructure and in the height of the funnel. Early units have only a twin 30mm mounting forward of the bridge and no FC director; later versions have 30mm mountings at both ends of the superstructure and a Drum Tilt director at the base of the mast. Launchers for bombardment rockets are mounted on the fore-deck.

Above: BTR-60PB amphibious personnel carriers come ashore from a Polnocny-class landing ship.

Below: Profile of a Polnocny II. The tall funnel distinguishes it from the Polnocny III.

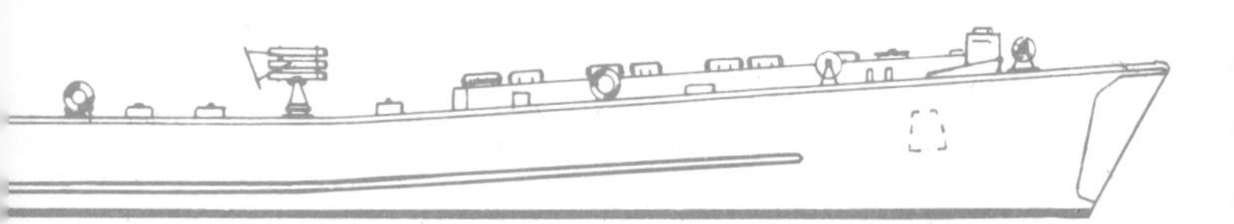

AIR CUSHION LANDING CRAFT

Aist

Completed: 1975 onward, Leningrad.
No. in class: 12.
Weight: 220t full load.
Dimensions: 157 x 57ft (48 x 18m).
Propulsion: Two gas-turbines; 24,000bhp = 65kt.
Armament: Four 30mm (2x2).

The Aist is the Soviet Navy's first large military hovercraft. Unlike the experimental ACVs currently undergoing trials for the US Navy, it is not designed to be accommodated in the docking wells of larger landing ships, but is intended for independent high-speed assault operations over relatively short distances. Such a craft would clearly be extremely useful in the Baltic, where it would be invulnerable to defensive minefields laid by the Danish and Federal German navies to protect their respective coastlines.

The Aist is powered by two marinised gas-turbines, each rated at 12-14,000hp. The turbines drive four axial lift fans and four propeller units, giving a maximum speed estimated at 65kt (120km/h). A continuous tank deck with ramps at either end can accommodate two MBTs (T-62 or T-72) or five PT-76 amphibious tanks. A reduction in the number of vehicles enables up to 150 troops to be carried.

Right: An ACV of the Aist class at speed.

Below: Bow view of an Aist. Note the twin 30mm on either side of the bridge.

Above the vehicle hangar is a navigating bridge with good all-round vision and a lattice mast carrying the navigational radar. Twin 30mm mountings are fitted side by side at the forward end of the hangar and the Drum Tilt FC director is installed atop the bridge. As well as providing anti-aircraft defence, the guns can be used for the suppression of shore defences.

AIR CUSHION LANDING CRAFT

Lebed

Completed: 1967 onward.
No. in class: 10.
Weight: 85t full load.
Dimensions: 79 x 39ft (24 x 12m).
Propulsion: Two horizontal thrust engines, 7,200hp = 50kt; one vertical lift engine, 350hp.

Above: A Lebed, with the large bow ramp clearly visible.

AIR CUSHION LANDING CRAFT

Gus

Completed: 1970, Gorky.
No. in class: 33.
Weight: 27t full load.
Dimensions: 70 x 27ft (21 x 8m).
Propulsion: Two horizontal thrust engines, 1,560hp = 58kt. one vertical thrust engine, 780bhp.

The Gus class entered series production in the early 1970s. Adapted from a 50-seater civilian craft, the Gus can carry 24 fully-equipped troops but no vehicles. It can be used either for direct assault or for rapid reinforcement, complementing the larger vehicle-carrying ACVs of the Aist class. Gus craft serve in every Soviet fleet except the Northern Fleet.

Below: The Gus-class ACV is a naval version of a civilian craft. It can carry troops but not heavy equipment.

Trials with the experimental Lebed class ACV began in the late 1960s. Pre-production models had a pointed nose, with the bridge inside the forward end of the large cabin which formed their upperworks. The production craft built towards the end of the 1970s, however, have a broad bow ramp and a raised control cab to starboard, with a twin 30mm AA mounting to port. This arrangement has created enough internal volume for an alternative loading of one or two PT-76 amphibious tanks, 120 troops, or 45 tons of cargo. It appears that the production units have been specially designed to operate from the docking-well of the *Ivan Rogov*.

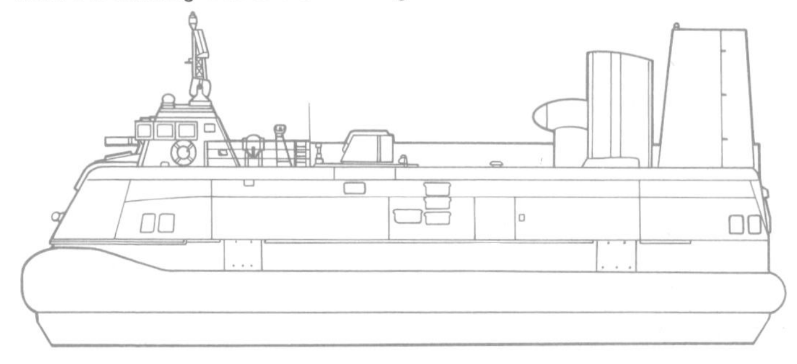

Above: Profile of the Lebed-class ACV.

Above: An assault by Naval Infantry using a Gus-class ACV with helicopter support.

Support Ships

The remote situation of many Soviet bases has made necessary the construction of large numbers of Depot Ships (*Plavuchaya Baza,* PB) and Repair Ships (*Plavuchaya Masterskaya,* PM). Where the Soviets have acquired basing rights in foreign countries, they have tended not to invest heavily in fixed installations; this has reinforced the requirement for vessels to provide the necessary supplies and maintenance facilities for their surface ships and submarines.

Underway replenishment lagged behind the West until the early 1970s, when specialized Fleet Oilers (*Voyeny Tanker,* VTA) began to appear. The year 1978 saw the completion of the first unit of a new class designed to carry large quantities of dry stores in addition to fuel oil and fresh water: she is designated Fleet Replenishment Ship (*Voyeny Transport,* VTR).

DEPOT SHIP/PB

Amga

Completed: 1973 onward, unknown yards.
Names: *Amga, Vetluga* (+ 1 building).
Displacement: 4,800t standard; 5,800t full load.
Dimensions: 335 oa x 59 x 14ft (102 x 18 x 4.5m).
Propulsion: 2-shaft diesels; 4,000bhp = 12kt.
Armament: Four 25mm (2x2).

Above: The replenishment tanker *Boris Chilikin* refuels a BRK and a BPK of the Kashin class in the Mediterranean.

As completed these vessels were manned by naval personnel, but several have been repainted in mercantile colours and are manned by civilians.

The Amga class ships serve as tenders to the Soviet ballistic missile submarines (SSBN). The design centres on a long, narrow hangar served by a massive crane with a reach of 112ft (34m) and an estimated capacity of 55 tons. The construction dates of the class suggest that the Amga was specifically designed to handle the 43ft (13m) SS-N-8 missiles of the Delta class submarines.

Below: *Amga,* showing the massive crane designed to handle SS-N-8 and SS-N-18 missiles that are part of the Soviet Union's ballistic missile force.

DEPOT or REPAIR SHIP/PB or PM

Lama

Completed: 1963-79, Black Sea.
Names: *General Riyabakov, Voronezh, PB-625, PM-44, PM-93, PM-131, PM-150.*
Displacement: 4,500t standard; 6,000t full load.
Dimensions: 370 oa x 49 x 14ft (113 x 15 x 4.5m).
Propulsion: 2-shaft diesels; 5,000bhp = 15kt.
Armament: Four/eight 57mm (1x4, 2x2 or 2x4).
Sensors: *Surveillance:* Slim Net *or* Strut Curve.
Fire Control: one/two Hawk Screech *or* two Muff Cob.

The Lama class vessels were built to serve as missile tenders to submarines and surface ships and to provide base and repair facilities. At least two of the seven Lamas are classified as Depot Ships (PB), the remainder being designated Repair Ships (PM).

A raised section of the hull, 98ft (30m) long and 14ft (4.5m) high, serves as a magazine for cruise missiles. The missiles are run out onto the well-deck forward of the magazine on wheeled dollies, for which twin railway tracks and turntables are provided. They are then transferred by the two 20-ton precision cranes located at the forward end of the magazine, which are normally stowed flat on the deck. Mooring points in the hull enable submarines and missile craft to tie up alongside.

There are considerable variations within the class in armament and fire control arrangements; the two Depot Ships have a number of further modifications to enable them to serve as tenders to the Nanuchka, Osa and

Above: A repair ship of the Lama class. The raised section of the hull houses the magazine for missile reloads.

Matka class missile boats. Because they need to handle missiles only up to the size of the 30ft (9m) SS-N-9, these two units have a shorter well-deck and smaller (10-ton) cranes. They can also be distinguished by their more extensive superstructures and taller funnels.

Below: The vessel depicted is one of two ships fitted to provide support facilities for missile boats.

SUBMARINE DEPOT SHIP/PB

Ugra

Completed: 1963-72, Nikolayev.
Names: *Ivan Kolyshkin, Ivan Kucherenko, Ivan Vakhrameev, Tobol, Volga.*
Displacement: 6,750t standard; 9,500t full load.
Dimensions: 453 oa x 58 x 20ft (141 x 18 x 6m).
Propulsion: 2-shaft diesels; 14,000bhp = 20kt.
Armament: Eight 57mm (4x2).
Sensors: *Surveillance:* Strut Curve.
Fire Control: two Muff Cob.

The Ugra class followed the Don class onto the slipways at Nikolayev. Modifications were made to the superstructure and to the armament, giving the Ugra an altogether more "modern" appearance than the Don, but the basic layout of the propulsion machinery, munitions stowage and even the cranage remained identical.

In place of the single 100mm gun of the Don, the Ugra has twin 57mm automatic mountings, with Muff Cob FC directors above the bridge and atop a short lattice structure aft. The after pair of mountings were positioned side by side to allow room for a helicopter platform. In the early 1970s, *Ivan Kolyshkin* was fitted with a helicopter hangar (between the after gun mountings) and a large raised helicopter platform. This modification has not been extended to other units.

Below: Profile of a training ship of the Ugra class. A tall deckhouse has been constructed aft on the former flight deck.

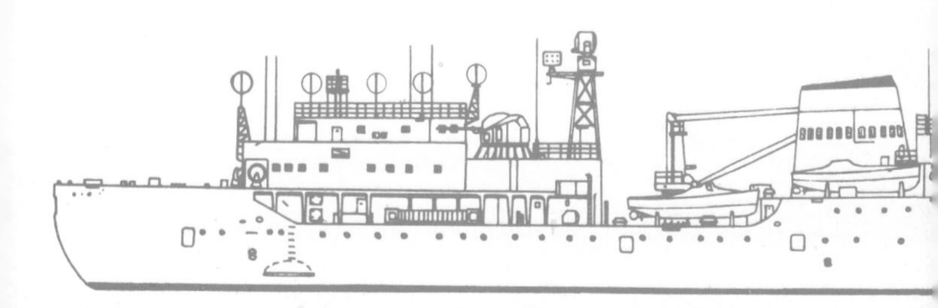

Above: An Ugra-class submarine depot ship underway off Hawaii.

Facilities for submarine support are similar to those of the Don class, the only visible modifications being an extra pair of mooring points aft and slightly larger (6-ton) cranes on either side of the torpedo hold forward of the bridge. Like their predecessors, the Ugra class frequently serve as flagships, and *Volga* has been fitted with a tall lattice mainmast carrying Vee Cone HF communications antennae. Two sister ships, *Gangut* and *Borodino,* serve as training ships.

Above: An Ugra-class submarine depot ship.

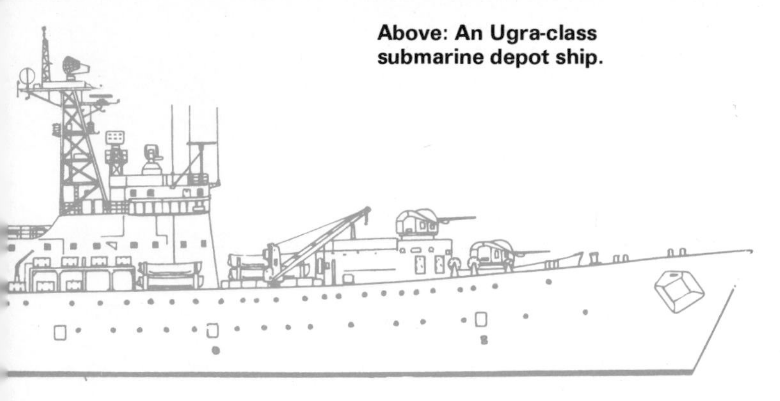

SUBMARINE DEPOT SHIP/PB

Don

Completed: 1958-62, Nikolayev.
Names: *Nikolai Stolbov, Dmitri Galkin, Fedor Vidyaev, Magadansky Komsomolets, Magomed Gadzhiev, Viktor Kotelnikov.*
Displacement: 6,730t standard; 9,000t full load.
Dimensions: 449 oa x 55 x 20ft (137 x 17 x 6m).
Propulsion: 2-shaft diesels; 14,000bhp = 21kt.
Armament: Four 100m (4x1); eight 57mm (4x2) (*see text*).
Sensors: *Surveillance:* Slim Net.
Fire Control: Sun Visor, two Hawk Screech.

The Don class vessels were built in the late 1950s to serve as depot ships for the growing force of Soviet submarines. Eight to twelve submarines can be supported at sea with fuel, provisions, fresh water and spare torpedoes. Repairs can also be undertaken and the extensive accommodation provided enables submarine crews to transfer while their boat is alongside.

The squared-off bow accommodates a lift-hook with a capacity of 100 tons, and there are mooring points for submarines in the sides of the hull forward and amidships. Aft of the funnel is a 10-ton crane for the transfer of spares, dry stores and torpedoes, and for the removal, if necessary, of rudders and propellers. Railway tracks run forward from this area outside the superstructure and terminate on either side of the torpedo hold forward of the bridge, which is itself served by two 5-ton cranes.

A substantial gun armament is fitted, with single 100mm guns and twin 57mm mountings disposed symmetrically fore and aft. *Magadansky Komsomolets* was completed with a helicopter platform in place of the after 100m mounting; this modification was extended to *Viktor Kotelnikov* (which lost both after mountings) in 1967.

Dmitri Galkin and *Fedor Vidyaev* have twin 25mm mountings abreast the bridge and mainmast. Their pole foremasts have been replaced by lattice masts. The Slim Net surveillance aerial has been moved to the new lattice foremast and Vee Cone HF communications antennae installed atop the mainmast. The latter modification emphasizes the role of the Soviet depot ships as flagships of their respective squadrons.

Above: A bow shot of a submarine depot ship of the Don class.

Above: An overhead view of *Dmitri Galkin,* showing the cranage and the heavy gun armament. Note the lattice foremast and the Vee Cone HF communications antennae atop the mainmast. These ships frequently serve as flagships of the Soviet submarine squadrons.

Left: This ship has the original Don class rig, but has had all 100mm guns and FC directors removed and a helicopter platform added aft. Note the heavy lift-hook.

FLEET REPLENISHMENT SHIP/VTR

Berezina

Completed: 1978, 61 Kommuna (Nikolayev).
Names: *Berezina.*
Displacement: 40,000t full load.
Dimensions: 686 oa x 79 x 36ft (209 x 24 x 11m).
Propulsion: 2-shaft diesels; 54,000bhp = 20-22kt.
Armament: *ASW:* two Hormone A helicopters; two RBU 1000 mortars.
AAW: twin SA-N-4 launcher (18 missiles); four 30mm gatlings.
Sensors: *Surveillance:* Strut Curve.
Fire Control: one Pop Group, one Muff Cob, two Bass Tilt.
Sonars: MF (?) hull-mounted.

Berezina has almost twice the capacity of any previous Soviet support ship. She caused a considerable stir in the West when she first appeared in 1979 because, although primarily a replenishment vessel, she is clearly much more besides. Her comprehensive armament, which enables her to conduct limited ASW operations and to defend herself against attack from the air, suggests possible employment as a base/command ship in distant areas such as the Indian Ocean. Her extensive accommodation includes berths not only for her own crew but also for the relief crews of submarines, for which there are mooring points along her sides.

For liquid replenishment there are single constant-tension stations port and starboard and a third refuelling point on the stern. Solid stores are transferred by sliding-stay constant-tension stations, two on either side. Four 10-ton cranes amidships can transfer stores to ships alongside. The two Hormone A helicopters are specially configured for vertical replenishment operations. Estimated capacity is 16,000 tons of Furnace-Fuel Oil (FFO) and diesel, 500 tons of water, and 3,000 tons of provisions, munitions and spares.

Forward of the bridge there are superimposed twin 57mm mountings. There is an SA-N-4 missile launcher above the hangar aft, with paired gatlings on either side. For ASW, two RBU 1000 mortars are fitted forward abreast the twin 57mm mountings, and the Hormone helicopters may be capable of antisubmarine operations in addition to their VERTREP role. The angle of the ship's stem suggests that a bow sonar is fitted.

Right: A bow view of *Berezina.* The RBU 1000 A/S mortars are mounted on either side of the twin 57mm mountings.

Below: *Berezina* is the Soviet Navy's largest and most heavily armed underway replenishment vessel.

FLEET OILER/VTA

Boris Chilikin

Completed: 1971-78, Baltiisky Yard (Leningrad).
Names: *Boris Butoma, Boris Chilikin, Dnestr, Genrik Gasanov, Ivan Bubnov, Vladimir Kolechitsky.*
Displacement: 24,500t full load.
Dimensions: 532 oa x 70 x 29ft (162 x 21 x 9m).
Propulsion: 1-shaft diesels; 9,600bhp = 16kt.
Armament: Removed from all ships (*see text*).

Boris Chilikin, completed in 1971, was the first Soviet naval tanker capable of abeam replenishment, previous vessels having used the slower and less efficient stern refuelling method. The construction of large specialized ships employing modern transfer techniques was seen at the time as an indication of the shift in Soviet naval strategy away from area defence and towards ocean-going operations.

Early units of the class had solid-stores constant-tension rigs on both sides forward, with stations for liquid replenishment amidships—two on either

Below: An overhead view of a replenishment oiler of the Chilikin class in Pacific waters.

Right: Underway replenishment in the Pacific. A Chilikin refuels a Rocket Cruiser of the Kynda class using the abeam method. Previously the Soviet Navy used the stern refuelling method. The technique implies that ocean-going operations are an important part of Soviet naval strategy

Above: A Chilikin-class oiler refuels a BPK of the Kashin class in the Mediterranean.

side–and at the stern. On later units the forward kingpost handles solid stores to starboard only and has a liquid replenishment station to port. Between the first and second kingposts is a two-storey deckhouse which serves as a logistics administration centre and as a control post for directing transfer operations at sea. There are three cranes for alongside replenishment: the two forward of the first kingpost have a capacity of 5 tons; the single crane aft has a capacity of 3 tons. Estimated capacity for the Chilikin class is 13,500 tons of FFO, diesel and fresh water; 400 tons of munitions; 400 tons of provisions; and 400 tons of stores.

The first four units were completed with two twin 57mm automatic mountings on the forecastle, a single Muff Cob FC director at the base of the mast, and a Strut Curve surveillance radar. *Ivan Bubnov* and *Genrik Gasanov*, however, were completed in merchant colours and carried no armament. The first four ships have now also transferred to merchant colours with civilian crews: all weapons and sensors have consequently been removed.

Weapons and Sensors

Ship-borne Aircraft

Yak-36 FORGER A
In Service: 1976.
Weight: 22,050lb (10,000kg) max.
Dimensions: 49 x 25 x 13ft (15 x 7.6 x 4m).
Single-seat subsonic VTOL naval attack aircraft deployed on Kiev class ASW cruisers. Two vertical lift engines behind cockpit in addition to main cruise/lift engine. Estimated 2,600lb (1,200kg) payload. Short range. May be interim type. Two-seat training version (Forger B) has length of 58ft (17.7m).

Ka-25 HORMONE A/B
In Service: 1967.
Weight: 15,500lb (7,000kg) max.
Length: 32ft (9.75m).
Height: 18ft (5.4m).
First Soviet ship-borne ASW helicopter, developed from Ka-15 and Ka-20. Co-axial rotors give exceptional lift capability at cost of height. Hormone A carries dipping sonar, MAD, sonobuoys, and has a weapons bay for two homing torpedoes or depth charges. Hormone B is a special electronics variant, distinguished by more spherical radome below nose, with Video Data Link to provide mid-course guidance to long-range cruise missiles on Kresta I, Kiev and Kirov classes.

Right: Two Yak-36 Forger VTOL aircraft on the flight deck of *Minsk*, the Kiev-class ASW cruiser.

Below: Profile of a Ka-25 Hormone A ASW helicopter. The quad Yagi array on the nose is called Home Guide by NATO.

Above: A Ka-25 Hormone A in flight. This example lacks both the flotation bags and the quad Yagi array seen on the helicopter at left.

Surveillance Radars

TOP SAIL
In Service: 1967.
Long-range (300nm, 555km) 3-D radar used to provide target data for SA-N-3 SAM system. Mounted back-to-back with long-range air search aerial in Top Pair installation on *Kirov*.

TOP STEER
In Service: 1976.
Smaller version of Top Sail. Employed to monitor air picture in Kievs and *Kirov*, and to provide height-finding data for SA-N-7 in *Sovremenny*.

BIG NET
In Service: 1965.
Long-range (100-200nm, 185-370km) air search radar installed in Kresta Is and some Kashins.

HEAD NET C
In Service: 1965.
V-beam 3-D radar comprising two Head Net A antennae mounted back-to-back at an angle of 30° to one another. Standard air search radar on major warships since the mid-1960s.

HEAD NET A
In Service: 1960.
Standard air surveillance radar on major warships in early 1960s. Effective range 60-70nm (110-130km).

STRUT CURVE
In Service: 1963.
Standard air surveillance radar on small warships and auxiliaries. Lightweight antenna. Effective range 60nm (110km). Back-to-back installation (Strut Pair) in *Bedovy* (Kildin class) and new ASW destroyers.

SLIM NET
In Service: 1955.
Standard air surveillance radar on small warships and auxiliaries until mid-1960s. Obsolescent.

Right: A Head Net C V-beam antenna on a BPK of the Kara class.

Far right: Central structure of the Rocket Cruiser *Kirov*. The Top Pair array is mounted on the main radar tower and a second 3-D radar, Top Steer, is located on the smaller tower aft.

Above: The main radar installation of *Minsk* comprises Top Sail (right) and Top Steer (left) 3-D antennae. Between them is a carrier-controlled approach radar designated Top Knot in the NATO system of identification.

Surface-to-Air Missiles

SA-N-1 GOA
In Service: 1962.
Length: 20ft (6.1m).
Range: 17nm (30km).
Fire Control: Peel Group.
Guidance: Command.
Twin launcher. Magazine holds 22 missiles. Installed in most major combatants completed or converted during 1960s.

SA-N-3 GOBLET
In Service: 1967.
Length: 20ft (6.1m).
Range: 20nm (35km).
Fire Control: Head Lights.
Guidance: Command.
Twin launcher. Early models had four reload hatches, later models only two. Magazine holds 22 missiles. Installed in most major combatants completed in 1970s.

SA-N-4
In Service: 1969.
Length: 11.5ft (3.5m).
Range: 6nm (10km).
Fire Control: Pop Group.
Guidance: Command.
Twin "pop-up" launcher in cylindrical bin containing 18 reloads. Installed as primary anti-air system in some small combatants and as secondary system in major combatants.

SA-N-5
In Service: late 1970s.
Length: 4.4ft (1.35m).
Range: 5nm (8km).
Guidance: Infra-Red Homing.
Adapted from land-based SA-7. Quadruple ready-use launcher. Now being fitted to amphibious vessels and some small combatants.

SA-N-6
In Service: 1980.
Length: 19.5ft (6m) (?).
Range: 30nm (50km).
Fire Control: Top Globe.
Guidance: Track-Via-Missile (TVM).
Vertical launch from hatches in deck. Trials in *Azov* (Kara class) and installed in *Kirov*.

SA-N-7
In Service: 1981-82 (?).
Length: 14.8-16.4ft (4.5-5m) (?).
Range: 15nm (25km).
Fire Control: (?)
Guidance: Semi-Active.
Single launcher similar to US Navy's Tartar. Trials in *Provorny* (Kashin class) for installation aboard new destroyers.

Above: An SA-N-1 Goa missile launched from a BPK of the Kashin class. The boost fins of the missile are not quite fully deployed in this view.

Left: A rare picture of an SA-N-4 launch from a Koni of the East German Navy. The SA-N-4 has been installed in over 100 vessels, ranging in size from missile boats to the largest cruisers.

Below: The after part of a Krivak, showing the "bin" containing the SA-N-4 launcher (A). B is the Owl Screech fire control radar for the twin 76mm guns fitted aft.

Surface-to-Surface Missiles

SS-N-2 STYX
In Service: 1959.
Length: 20.5ft (6.25m).
Range: 20-25nm (37-46km).
Guidance: Radar and IR Homing.
"A" and "B" models on Osa-class missile boats. "C" version with improved homing on Kashin-Mod., Kildin and latest FPBs.

SS-N-3 SHADDOCK
In Service: 1962.
Length: 36ft (10.9m).
Range: 170nm (315km).
Fire Control: Scoop Pair.
In quadruple or paired launchers on RKRs. Relay aircraft needed beyond horizon range.

SS-N-9 SIREN
In Service: 1969.
Length: 30ft (9.2m).
Range: 60-90nm (110-170km).
Fire Control: Band Stand.
In triple elevating launchers on Nanuchka; paired launchers on Sarancha. Relay aircraft needed beyond horizon range.

SS-N-12
In Service: 1976.
Length: 38ft (11.5m) (?).
Range: 250nm (460km).
Fire Control: Trap Door.
Successor to SS-N-3. In paired elevating launchers on Kievs and possibly on new RKRs currently under construction in Black Sea.

SS-N-19
In Service: 1980.
Length: 33ft (10m) (?).
Range: 200nm (370km) (?).
Fire Control: (?).
Vertical launch from hatches in *Kirov*.

Above: The quadruple launch tubes for the SS-N-3 missile aboard a Rocket Cruiser of the Kynda class.

Below: Twin launchers for SS-N-12 missiles on *Kiev.* The launcher for SA-N-3 can also be seen.

Below left: An SS-N-2 Styx missile being loaded aboard a missile boat of the Komar class. Note the large ventral booster.

Below: Triple launchers for SS-N-9 missiles on a missile boat of the Nanuchka class.

Antisubmarine Weapons

Missiles

FRAS-1
In Service: 1967.
Length: 20ft (6m) approx.
Range: 16nm (30km).
Payload: Nuclear warhead.
Fired from twin SUW-N-1 launcher on PKRs

SS-N-14
In Service: 1970.
Length: 23ft (7m) approx.
Range: 4 to 25nm (7 to 46km).
Payload: Homing torpedo.
Fired from quadruple launchers on BPKs and from twin reloadable launcher on Kirov Missile can be guided in flight.

Rockets

RBU 1200
In Service: 1955.
Range: 4,000ft (1,200m).
Two horizontal rows of barrels superimposed three on two. Tubes elevate but fixed in train. Manual reloading.

RBU 2500
In Service: 1957.
Range: 8,200ft (2,500m).
Two horizontal rows of eight barrels. Can be trained and elevated. Manual reloading.

RBU 6000
In Service: 1962.
Range: 20,000ft (6,000m).
Twelve barrels in horseshoe configuration, fired in paired sequence. Can be trained and elevated. Automatic reloading.

Right: Rockets from an RBU 1200 mortar fired by a patrol craft of the East German Navy. The three/two barrel arrangement can be seen here.

Left: An RBU 6000 12-barrelled mortar on a BPK of the Kashin class. The twelve barrels are arranged in a horseshoe configuration.

Above: A quadruple launcher for SS-N-14. antisubmarine missiles aboard a BPK of the Kresta II class.

Left: A six-barrelled RBU 1000 mortar. This launcher can be both trained in azimuth and elevated.

RBU 1000
In Service: 1963.
Range: 3,300ft (1,000m).
Six barrels arranged in two vertical rows of three and fired in order. Can be trained and elevated. Automatic reloading. **RBU 600** has similar configuration but has shorter range and manual reloading.

Guns (since 1960)

100mm (single)
In Service: 1976.
Fire Control: Kite Screech.
Dual purpose weapon on Krivak II. *Kirov* and *Udaloy.*

76mm (single)
In Service: 1977.
Fire Control: Bass Tilt.
Dual-purpose weapon on recent missile boats.

76mm (twin)
In Service: 1962.
Fire Control: Hawk Screech/Owl Screech.
Dual-purpose weapon installed on many major warships since Kynda class.

57mm (twin)
In Service: 1963.
Fire Control: Muff Cob.
Standard medium-calibre AA weapon installed on both large and small warships.

30mm (twin)
In Service: 1961.
Fire Control: Drum Tilt.
Standard small AA weapon on minesweepers, FPBs, and Kotlin-SAM and Kanin conversions.

30mm (gatling)
In Service: 1970.
Fire Control: Bass Tilt.
Six-barrelled anti-missile weapon on all major combatants since 1970, and on many recent smaller craft.

Right: A twin 57mm automatic mounting on a Nanuchka class Small Rocket Ship.

Below: Single 100mm mountings aboard the Rocket Cruiser *Kirov.*

Right: A twin 30mm mounting on a fast patrol boat. A decontamination monitoring operator is assessing the radiological level on the mounting as part of his practice drill. NBC readiness is a very important element in Soviet naval training, and suggest that Soviet ships are designed for a nuclear environment.

PRINTED IN BELGIUM BY

145